First World War
and Army of Occupation
War Diary
France, Belgium and Germany

39 DIVISION
Divisional Troops
Royal Army Medical Corps
Divisional Field Ambulance Workshop Unit,
82 Sanitary Section,
50 Mobile Veterinary Section
4 March 1916 - 30 March 1916

WO95/2579/2-4

The Naval & Military Press Ltd
www.nmarchive.com
Published in association with The National Archives

Published by

The Naval & Military Press Ltd

Unit 10 Ridgewood Industrial Park,

Uckfield, East Sussex,

TN22 5QE England

Tel: +44 (0) 1825 749494

www.naval-military-press.com

www.nmarchive.com

This diary has been reprinted in facsimile from the original. Any imperfections are inevitably reproduced and the quality may fall short of modern type and cartographic standards.

© **Crown Copyright**
Images reproduced by permission of The National Archives, London, England, 2015.

Contents

Document type	Place/Title	Date From	Date To
Heading	WO95/2579 Div Field Ambulance Workshop Unit Mar 1916		
Heading	39th Division Medical Divl Fd Amb. W' Shop Unit Mar 1916		
Heading	War Diary of 39th Divisional Field Ambulance 2 Workshop Unit From 4th March to 30th March 1916		
War Diary	Rouen	04/03/1916	08/03/1916
War Diary	Rouen Abbeville	09/03/1916	09/03/1916
War Diary	Abbeville Morbecque	10/03/1916	10/03/1916
War Diary	Morbecque Estaires	11/03/1916	11/03/1916
War Diary	Doulieu	12/03/1916	14/03/1916
War Diary	Estaires	15/03/1916	25/03/1916
War Diary	Estaires Calonne St. Venant	26/03/1916	26/03/1916
War Diary	St Venant Lestrem	27/03/1916	27/03/1916
War Diary	Lestrem	28/03/1916	30/03/1916
Heading	WO95/2579/3 82 Sanitary Section Mar 1916-Mar 1917		
Heading	39th Division Medical 82nd Sanitary Section Mar 1916-1917 Mar		
Heading	39th Div. 82nd Sany Section. March		
War Diary	Morbecque	14/03/1916	26/03/1916
War Diary	St Vennant	27/03/1916	30/03/1916
War Diary	Morbecque	14/03/1916	26/03/1916
War Diary	St. Vennant	27/03/1916	30/03/1916
Heading	No 82 Sanitary Section April 1916		
War Diary	St Venant	01/04/1916	16/04/1916
War Diary	Locon	17/04/1916	30/04/1916
War Diary	St. Venant	01/04/1916	30/04/1916
Miscellaneous	D.A.G. 3rd Echelon Base.	02/06/1916	02/06/1916
Heading	39th Div. No. 82 Sanitary Section May 1916		
War Diary	Locon	01/05/1916	31/05/1916
Heading	No. 82 San. Section. June 1916		
War Diary	Locon	01/06/1916	30/06/1916
Heading	To The D.A.G. At The Base		
Heading	39th Division 82nd Sanitary Section July 1916		
War Diary	Locon	01/07/1916	07/07/1916
War Diary	Bethune	08/07/1916	14/07/1916
War Diary	Locon	15/07/1916	31/07/1916
Heading	82 Sanitary Section From 1-8-16-31-8-16 & 1-9-16-30-9-16		
Heading	War Diary of The 82nd Sanitary Section R.A.M.C.T. From 1st August 1916 to 31st August 1916 Volume 6		
War Diary	Locon	01/08/1916	11/08/1916
War Diary	Lozinghem	12/08/1916	12/08/1916
War Diary	Roellecourt	13/08/1916	31/08/1916
War Diary	War Diary of The 82nd Sanitary Section R.A.M.C.T. From 1st September 1916 to 30th September 1916 Volume 7		
War Diary	Acheux	01/09/1916	30/09/1916
Heading	A.D.M.S. 39th Div.	01/01/1917	01/01/1917

Heading	War Diary of The 82nd Sanitary Section R.A.M.C.T. From 1st October 1916 to 31st October 1916 Volume 8		
War Diary	Acheux	01/10/1916	04/10/1916
War Diary	Englebelmer	05/10/1916	12/10/1916
War Diary	Bouzincourt	13/10/1916	31/10/1916
Heading	39th Div. 82nd. Sanitary Section Nov. 1916		
Heading	War Diary Of The 82nd Sanitary Section R.A.M.C.I. From 1st November 1916 To 30th November 1916 Volume 9		
War Diary	Bouzincourt	01/11/1916	16/11/1916
War Diary	Beauval	17/11/1916	18/11/1916
War Diary	Esquelbecq	19/11/1916	30/11/1916
Heading	A.D.M.S. 39th Div.	00/11/1916	00/11/1916
Heading	39th Div. War Diary of The 82nd Sanitary Section R.A.M.C.I. From 1st December 1916 to 31st December 1916 Volume 10		
War Diary	Esquelbecq	01/12/1916	13/12/1916
War Diary	Peselhoek	14/12/1916	31/12/1916
Miscellaneous	A.D.M.S. 39th Div.	01/01/1917	01/01/1917
Heading	War Diary of The 82nd Sanitary Section R.A.M.C.T. From 1st January 1917 to 31st January 1917 Volume 11		
War Diary	Peselhoek	01/01/1917	15/01/1917
War Diary	Poperinghe	16/01/1917	31/01/1917
Heading	39th Div. War Diary Of The 82nd Sanitary Section R.A.M.C. (T). From 1st February 1917 To 28th February 1917 Volume 12		
Heading	A.D.M.S. 39th Division.	01/03/1917	01/03/1917
War Diary		19/02/1917	28/02/1917
Heading	39th Div. War Diary Of The 82nd Sanitary Section R.A.M.C. (T) From 1st March 1917 To 31st March 1917 Volume 13		
War Diary	Waratah Camp (G 15.a.6.9 Sheet 28)	04/03/1917	11/03/1917
War Diary	Waratah Camp G15. a 69	12/03/1917	17/03/1917
War Diary	G 15 A. 72	18/03/1917	23/03/1917
War Diary	Waratah Camp G 15.a.72	24/03/1917	25/03/1917
Miscellaneous	39th. Division. Appendix No. 1	01/03/1917	01/03/1917
Heading	WO95/2579/4 50 Mobile Veterinary Section Mar 1916-Jan 1919		
Heading	39th Division 50th Mobile Vety Secn Mar 1916-Jan 1919		
Heading	50 M Vol Sec Vol 1 Mar 16 Jan 19		
War Diary	Left Witley	04/03/1916	04/03/1916
War Diary	Southampton	04/03/1916	04/03/1916
War Diary	Arrived Harve	08/03/1916	08/03/1916
War Diary	Left Harve	09/03/1916	09/03/1916
War Diary	Arrived Steenbecque	10/03/1916	30/03/1916
War Diary	Merville	04/02/1916	17/04/1916
War Diary	Locon	17/04/1916	13/08/1916
War Diary	Le Quesnill	18/08/1916	23/08/1916
War Diary	Le Brevillers	24/08/1916	24/08/1916
War Diary	Brevillers	25/08/1916	25/08/1916
War Diary	St Leger	28/08/1916	28/08/1916
War Diary	Acheux	30/08/1916	30/09/1916
War Diary	Acheux	01/09/1916	03/10/1916
War Diary	Hedauville.	05/10/1916	08/10/1916
War Diary	Bouzincourt	11/10/1916	14/10/1916

Type	Location	Start	End
War Diary	Hedauville Bouzincourt	18/10/1916	28/10/1916
War Diary	Bouzincourt	02/11/1916	16/11/1916
War Diary	Esquelbecq.	19/11/1916	15/12/1916
War Diary	Water	19/12/1916	30/01/1917
War Diary	Poperinghe	03/02/1917	20/02/1917
War Diary	Ledringham	20/02/1917	28/02/1917
War Diary		27/02/1917	27/02/1917
War Diary		20/02/1917	20/02/1917
War Diary	Ledringham Poperinghe	01/03/1917	31/03/1917
War Diary	Poperinghe	03/04/1917	10/04/1917
War Diary	Herzeele	12/04/1917	31/05/1917
War Diary	Peselhoek	01/06/1917	29/06/1917
War Diary	Peselhoek	02/07/1917	31/07/1917
War Diary	Peselhoek	01/08/1917	07/08/1917
War Diary	Berthen	08/08/1917	14/08/1917
War Diary	La Clytte	15/08/1917	11/09/1917
War Diary	La Clytte	01/09/1917	28/09/1917
War Diary	St Jans Cappel	28/09/1917	16/10/1917
War Diary	Devises Camp	16/10/1917	31/10/1917
War Diary	Devises Camp	01/11/1917	28/11/1917
War Diary	Water	29/11/1917	30/11/1917
War Diary	Water	01/12/1917	09/12/1917
War Diary	Nielles-Lez-Belgium	11/12/1917	31/12/1917
War Diary	St Momelin	31/12/1917	02/01/1918
War Diary	A 28 C. 2.6	03/01/1918	22/01/1918
War Diary	Proven	23/01/1918	26/01/1918
War Diary	Morcourt	29/01/1918	02/02/1918
War Diary	Nurlu	03/02/1918	28/03/1918
War Diary	Nurlu	01/03/1916	12/03/1916
War Diary	Haut Allaines	13/03/1918	03/04/1918
War Diary	Andainville	06/04/1918	06/04/1918
War Diary	Gamaches	08/04/1918	09/04/1918
War Diary	Arques	10/04/1918	11/04/1918
War Diary	Eperlecques-Estmont	12/04/1918	30/04/1918
War Diary	Eperlecques	01/05/1918	07/06/1918
War Diary	Rodelinghem	08/05/1918	14/05/1918
War Diary	Autingues	15/06/1918	13/07/1918
War Diary	Autingues	26/07/1918	17/08/1918
War Diary	Lumbres	18/08/1918	31/08/1918
War Diary	Lumbres	01/09/1918	10/09/1918
War Diary	St Omer	11/09/1918	30/09/1918
War Diary	Stavele	01/10/1918	14/10/1918
War Diary	Potijze	15/10/1918	21/10/1918
War Diary	Lendelede	22/10/1918	23/10/1918
War Diary	Lendelede	24/10/1918	31/10/1918
Miscellaneous	D.A.G. G.H.Q. 3 Echelon		
War Diary	Le Chat	01/11/1918	07/11/1918
War Diary	Lauwe	08/11/1918	23/11/1918
War Diary	Tattingham	24/11/1918	30/11/1918
Miscellaneous	D.A.G. G.H.Q. 3 Echelon	31/12/1918	31/12/1918
War Diary	Tattingham	01/12/1918	31/12/1918
War Diary	D.A.G. G.H.Q. 3 Echelon	09/02/1919	09/02/1919
War Diary	Tatingham Strazeele La Madeleine	01/01/1919	13/01/1919
War Diary	La Madeleine	14/01/1919	31/01/1919

② WO95/2579

DIV Field Ambulance Workshop Unit

Mar 1916

39TH DIVISION
MEDICAL

DIVL FD AMB. W'SHOP UNIT

MAR 1916

39TH DIVISION
MEDICAL

<u>CONFIDENTIAL</u>

WAR DIARY OF :-

39th DIVISIONAL FIELD AMBULANCE & WORKSHOP UNIT.

FROM 4th MARCH to 30th MARCH 1916

COMMITTEE FOR THE
MEDICAL HISTORY OF THE WAR

Date   9 - JUN 016

WAR DIARY
or
INTELLIGENCE SUMMARY.

39th DIVISIONAL F.A.W.U. SHEET L.

Army Form C. 2118.

(Erase heading not required.)

Place	Date	Hour	Summary of Events and Information	Remarks and references to Appendices
ROUEN	4/3/16	6 P.M.	Unit arrived overseas from Southampton by S.S. ARCHANGEL	
ROUEN	5/3/16		1 Workshop 1 Stores wagon 1 30 cwt-lorry 1 SUNBEAM light-car 15 SUNBEAM ambulances 6 FORD ambulances + 3 motor cycles arrived at Rouen unit by S.S. SORRENTO	
ROUEN	6/3/16		Unloading lorries, cars, + ambulances.	
ROUEN	7/3/16		Repairing damage to vehicles caused by rough passage + careless embarkation	
ROUEN	8/3/16	4.15 P.M.	Inspection by A.D.T. Drew 2 more motor cycles under orders of A.D.T. Received orders to proceed to ABBEVILLE on following day.	
ROUEN ABBEVILLE	9/3/16	8 A.M.	Left Rouen for ABBEVILLE _ ROUTE VERT GALANT _ ST MARTIN _ OMONVILLE _ NEUFCHATEL _ BLANGY _ ABBEVILLE _ 98 KILOMETRES	
ABBEVILLE MORBECQUE	10/3/16	8 AM	Left ABBEVILLE for MORBECQUE _ ROUTE _ HESDIN _ FRUGES _ THEROUANNE _ AIRE _ STEENBECQUE _ MORBECQUE _ 95 = 60 KILOMETRES. Handed over ambulances to 132nd, 133rd & 134th Field Ambulances	
MORBECQUE ESTAIRES	11/3/16	6.30 AM	Left MORBECQUE for ESTAIRES _ arrived at ESTAIRES + was ordered by Divn Major to proceed to DOULIEU _	

WAR DIARY
INTELLIGENCE SUMMARY.
(Erase heading not required.)

39th DIVISIONAL F.A.W.U. Army Form C. 2118.

SHEET II.

Instructions regarding War Diaries and Intelligence Summaries are contained in F. S. Regs., Part II. and the Staff Manual respectively. Title pages will be prepared in manuscript.

Place	Date	Hour	Summary of Events and Information	Remarks and references to Appendices
DOULIEU	12/3/16		Cleaning cars and doing minor repairs	
DOULIEU	13/3/16		Same as on previous day	
DOULIEU	14/3/16		Same as on 12th	
ESTAIRES	15/3/16	10 AM	Arrived at ESTAIRES	
ESTAIRES	16/3/16		Took over the Divisional Baths at ESTAIRES. Overhauling engine & dynamo.	
ESTAIRES	17/3/16		Overhauling engine & dynamo of Divisional Baths	
ESTAIRES	18/3/16		Same as on 14th	
ESTAIRES	19/3/16		Work on engine & dynamo completed	
ESTAIRES	20/3/16		Started boiler for Divisional Baths.	

WAR DIARY 39th DIVISIONAL F.A.W.U.
INTELLIGENCE SUMMARY.
SHEET No. III

Army Form C. 2118.

(Erase heading not required.)

Place	Date	Hour	Summary of Events and Information	Remarks and references to Appendices
ESTAIRES	21/3/16		Repairs to ambulances of Units.	
ESTAIRES	22/3/16		Same as on the 21st	
ESTAIRES	23/3/16		Same as on the 21st	
ESTAIRES	24/3/16		Inspected 132nd Field Ambulance	
ESTAIRES	25/3/16		Repairs to ambulances & motor cycles of Units	
ESTAIRES CALONNE ST VENANT	26/3/16	8.30 AM	Left ESTAIRES for CALONNE under orders from A.D.M.S. was then ordered to proceed to ST VENANT	
ST VENANT LESTREM	27/3/16	6 AM	Left ST VENANT for LESTREM	
LESTREM	28/3/16		Erecting shelters for Workshops & Blacksmiths Shop. Installing electric light for D.H.Q. at Chateau	Woolf 2/Lt ASC Joining 39 D.F.A.W.U.
LESTREM	29/3/16		Inspected the 133rd Field Ambulance	Walker to D IV F.A.W.U.
LESTREM	30/3/16		On this date F.A.W.U. is abolished under G.R.O. 1484.	R Walker O.C. 39th

(3)

WO95/2579
82 Sanitary Section
Mes 1916 – Mar 1917

39TH DIVISION
MEDICAL

82ND SANITARY SECTION
MAR 1916 - ~~DEC 1916~~
1917 MAR

To 2 ARMY

39th Div 17

82nd Army Section

Mar '16
Dec '16

Army Form C. 2118.

WAR DIARY
or
INTELLIGENCE SUMMARY.

(Erase heading not required.)

Sanitary Section 82.

Place	Date	Hour	Important orders received.	Daily situation.	Summary of Events and Information operations in connection with our Field units operations in our Labour Coys.	Change of Strength	Nature of Field works constructed	Remarks and references to Appendices
MORBECQUE.	14/3/16			MORBECQUE and neighbourhood occupied by 39th Division.	Sanitary Supervision of Camps & Billets.		Incinerators, Latrines, grease-traps, etc.	
"	15/3/16			"	"		"	
"	16/3/16			"	"		"	
"	17/3/16			"	"		"	
"	18/3/16			"	"		"	
"	19/3/16			"	"		"	
"	20/3/16			"	"		"	
"	21/3/16			"	"		"	
"	22/3/16			"	"		"	
"	23/3/16			"	"		"	
"	24/3/16			"	"		"	
"	25/3/16			"	"		"	Hospital Charters
"	26/3/16		To move to ST VENNANT to take over Baths, Laundries etc on 27th	"	"		"	
ST VENNANT.	27/3/16			ST VENNANT.	Supervision of Baths and construction of Laundries, Drying Rooms etc.			
"	28/3/16							1 Entered, 3 men depart for BETHUNE

Charles W. Arthur Lieut.
Oc 82nd San. Sect.

Army Form C. 2118.

WAR DIARY
INTELLIGENCE SUMMARY.
(Erase heading not required.)

Instructions regarding War Diaries and Intelligence Summaries are contained in F. S. Regs., Part II. and the Staff Manual respectively. Title pages will be prepared in manuscript.

Place	Date	Hour	Important orders received.	Daily Situation / Summary of Events and Information / Operation with other units in neighbourhood.	Change of Strength	Nature of Field works constructed.	Remarks and references to Appendices
St Venant.	29/3/16		—	St Venant. Supervision of Baths, construction of Laundries	strength 20 depleted n/28	Incinerators, grease traps etc.	
"	30/3/16		—	"	"	"	

Dublin

Army Form C. 2118.

WAR DIARY
or
INTELLIGENCE SUMMARY.
(Erase heading not required.)

Sanitary Section 82

Instructions regarding War Diaries and Intelligence Summaries are contained in F. S. Regs., Part II. and the Staff Manual respectively. Title pages will be prepared in manuscript.

Place	Date	Hour	Important orders received	Daily Situation	Summary of Events and Information Operations in connection with other units in neighbourhood	Change of Strength	Nature of Field works constructed	Remarks and references to Appendices
MORBECQUE	14/3/16			MORBECQUE and neighbourhood accupies of 39th Division	Sanitary Supervision	—	Incinerators,	
"	15/3/16				Sanitary Supervision of Camps & Billets	—	Latrines, grease traps, etc.	
"	16/3/16			"	"	—	"	
"	17/3/16			"	"	—	"	
"	18/3/16			"	"	—	"	
"	19/3/16			"	"	—	"	
"	20/3/16			"	"	—	"	
"	21/3/16			"	"	—	"	
"	22/3/16			"	"	—	"	
"	23/3/16			"	"	—	"	
"	24/3/16			"	"	—	"	
"	25/3/16			"	"	—	"	Inspection of Lines
"	26/3/16		To move to ST VENNANT to take over Baths and Laundries etc in 27th	"	"	—	"	
ST. VENNANT	27/3/16			ST. VENNANT	Supervision of Baths and Construction of Laundries Drying Room etc.	—		
"	28/3/16			"	"	—		1 Corporal, 3 men depot for BETHUNE

Charles Kilby Cpt
R.A.M.C.
1/4/16

Army Form C. 2118.

WAR DIARY
INTELLIGENCE SUMMARY.
(Erase heading not required.)

Instructions regarding War Diaries and Intelligence Summaries are contained in F. S. Regs., Part II. and the Staff Manual respectively. Title pages will be prepared in manuscript.

Place	Date	Hour	Important orders received	Daily situation	Summary of Events and Information operations in connection with other units in neighbourhood.	Change of Strength.	Nature of Field works constructed	Remarks and references to Appendices
ST. VENNANT.	29/3/		—	ST VENNANT.	Supervision of Baths — Construction of Laundries.	Strength as deplater 28.2.	Incinerators from taps — etc.	
	30/3/		—	"				

No 82 Sanitary Section

COMMITTEE FOR THE
MEDICAL HISTORY OF THE WAR
Date 26 JUN 1916

WAR DIARY
or
INTELLIGENCE SUMMARY.
(Erase heading not required.)

Army Form C. 2118.

82ND SANITARY SECTION
39TH. DIVISION

Vol 2

Instructions regarding War Diaries and Intelligence Summaries are contained in F. S. Regs., Part II. and the Staff Manual respectively. Title pages will be prepared in manuscript.

Place	Date	Hour	IMPORTANT ORDERS RECEIVED	Summary of Events and Information			Remarks and references to Appendices
				DAILY SITUATION	OPERATIONS IN CONNECTION WITH OTHER UNITS IN NEIGHBOURHOOD	CHANGE OF STRENGTH	NATURE OF FIELD WORKS CONSTRUCTED
ST VENANT.	APRIL 1916 1			ST VENANT and area occupied by 39th Div	Sanitary supervision of Billets in divisional area. Supervision of St VENANT: Baths, construction of Laundry &c.	1 N.C.O. & 2 men detached for work at MERVILLE.	Incinerators, Latrines, Grease traps, etc.
	2			"	"		"
	3			"	"		"
	4			"	"		"
	5			"	"		"
	6			"	"		"
	7			"	Supervision of Baths, Laundry, Drying Room handed over to War Cookery 133rd F. Amb.		"
	8			"			"
	9			"	Sanitary Supervision of Billets		"
	10			"	"		"
	11			"	"	1 Pt. (Attached at ESTREM) evacuated to No 7 Genl H.P. Mallassises	"
	12			"	"		"
	13			"	"		"
	14			"	"		"
	15			"	"		"

O.C. 82ND SANITARY SECTION
LIEUT. R.A.M.C. T.

WAR DIARY
or
INTELLIGENCE SUMMARY.
(Erase heading not required.)

82ND SANITARY SECTION
39TH. DIVISION
Army Form C. 2118.

Instructions regarding War Diaries and Intelligence Summaries are contained in F. S. Regs., Part II. and the Staff Manual respectively. Title pages will be prepared in manuscript.

Place	Date	Hour	Summary of Events and Information				Remarks and references to Appendices
			IMPORTANT ORDERS RECEIVED	DAILY SITUATION	OPERATIONS IN CONNECTION WITH OTHER UNITS IN NEIGHBOURHOOD	CHANGE OF STRENGTH	NATURE OF FIELD WORKS CONSTRUCTED
	APRIL 1916						
ST VENANT.	16		Orders to move to MESPLAUX on 17th.	ST VENANT.	Sanitary supervision of billets of 39th divisional area.	1. N.C.O. & 2 men returned from MERVILLE.	
LOCON	17			MESPLAUX	Moved to MESPLAUX		
	18			MESPLAUX area occupied by 39th Divn.	Sanitary supervision of billets of divisional area.	1 Pte evacuated to 134th F. Amb. ✗	✗ subsequently to 20th C.C.S. STOMER.
	19		Became responsible for supply of Vermoral Powder.	"	"		
	20			"	"		
	21			"	"		
	22		Orders received changing responsibility for supply of Vermorel Powder to F. Amb.	"	"		
	23			"	"	Sick Pte rejoined unit from No 7 Gen. H.P. Mallassise.	
	24			"	"		
	25			"	"		
	26			"	"	1 Pte evacuated to F. Amb.	
	27			"	"	Received reinforcement 1. ASC(MT) Driver.	
	28			"	"	1 Pte evacuated to F. Amb.	
	29			"	"		
	30			"	"		

LIEUT. R.A.M.C. T.
O.C. 82ND SANITARY SECTION

Army Form C. 2118.

WAR DIARY
or
INTELLIGENCE SUMMARY.
(Erase heading not required.)

Instructions regarding War Diaries and Intelligence Summaries are contained in F. S. Regs., Part II. and the Staff Manual respectively. Title pages will be prepared in manuscript.

82nd SANITARY SECTION,
39th DIVISION.
Date 30.4.16

Vol 4

Place	Date	Hour	Important orders received	Daily situation	Operation in connection with other units in neighbourhood.	Change of strength	Nature of field works constructed.	Remarks and references to Appendices.
ST. VENANT.	April 1916. 1			St. Venant and area occupied by 39th Div.	Sanitary supervision of Billets in divisional area. Supervision of ST VENANT Baths, construction of laundry etc.	1 N.C.O. & 2 men detached for duties at MERVILLE. guard & p.o.	Incinerators, latrines, grease traps &c.	
	2			"	"		"	
	3			"	"		"	
	4			"	"		"	
	5			"	"		"	
	6			"	"		"	
	7			"	Supervision of Baths, Laundry & spraying room handed over to L-Corpl 337 Coy.		"	
	8			"	Sanitary supervision of Billets		"	
	9			"	"		"	
	10			"	"		"	
	11			"	"		"	
	12			"	"		"	1 Private attached LES'BŒUFS evacuated to No 7 Genl Hp Mallassises.
	13			"	"		"	
	14			"	"		"	
	15			"	"		"	

A.H.Wilson
LIEUT. R.A.M.C.
O.C. 82ND SANITARY SECTION

Army Form C. 2118.

82nd SANITARY SECTION.
39th DIVISION.
Date 30. 4. 16.

WAR DIARY
or
INTELLIGENCE SUMMARY.
(Erase heading not required.)

Instructions regarding War Diaries and Intelligence Summaries are contained in F. S. Regs., Part II. and the Staff Manual respectively. Title pages will be prepared in manuscript.

Place	Date	Hour	Summary of Events and Information			Remarks and references to Appendices
	April 1916.		Important orders received.	Daily situation	Operations in connection with other units in neighbourhood.	Change of Staff. Nature of Field works constructed.
ST VENANT.	16		Orders to move to MESPLAUX	ST VENANT		1 N.C.O. and 2 men returned from MERVILLE
	17			MESPLAUX.	Sanitary supervision of Billets of Divisional area	
	18			MESPLAUX and area occupied by 39th Div.	Moved to MESPLAUX. Sanitary supervision of Billets and area.	Inoculation returns received from the ×
	19		Became responsible for supply of Vermorel Powder.	"	"	1 Pte. evacuated to 134th F. Amb. ×
	20			"	"	
	21			"	"	
	22			"	"	
	23		Orders recd. changing responsibility for supply of Vermorel to F. Amb.	"	"	Sick parade reported unfit from No 7 Gen'l H. McAlister
	24			"	"	
	25			"	"	
	26			"	"	1 Pte evacuated to 7. Amb.
	27			"	"	Pte. reengagement / A.S.C. driver.
	28			"	"	1 Pte evacuated to 7. Amb.
	29			"	"	
	30			"	"	

× autographs to 20th C.C.S. St OMER

LIEUT. R.A.M.C. T.
O.C. 82ND SANITARY SECTION

"D.A.G. 3rd Echelon
  BASE.

Herewith fresh copy of War Diary of 82nd Sanitary Section.
There is a record of this diary having been posted on the 1° May 1916 & it is not understood why it has not reached its destination.

J M Porter Capt
for A.D.M.S 39
Divn

No. 82 Sanitary Section

39th Div

May 1916

COMMITTEE FOR THE
MEDICAL HISTORY OF THE WAR
Date   26 JUN. 1916

82 San Sec

Army Form C. 2118.

Vol 3

WAR DIARY
or
INTELLIGENCE SUMMARY.
(Erase heading not required.)

Instructions regarding War Diaries and Intelligence Summaries are contained in F.S. Regs., Part II. and the Staff Manual respectively. Title pages will be prepared in manuscript.

Place	Date	Hour	Important orders received.	Daily situation	Operations in connection with other units in neighbourhood.	Change of strength.	Nature of field works constructed.	Remarks and references to Appendices
LOCON.	1916 May. 1.			LOCON area occupied by 39th Division.	Sanitary Supervision of billets baths Laundries of thousand army inspection of Water Carts testing of Water Supplies	1 N.C.O. evacuated to Field Amb.	Lumatrines, Latrines, & urine traps etc.	
	2.			"	"	1 N.C.O man detached for work at Rulg du Vinage.	"	
	3.			"	"	1 Pte. Rejoined unit from F. Amb.	"	
	4.			"	"		"	
	5.			"	"	1 Pte. rejoined unit from F. Amb.	"	
	6.			"	"	1 N.C.O. rejoined from F. Amb.	"	
	7.			"	"	1 Coup rejoined unit from tank Base.	"	
	8.			"	"		"	
	9.			"	"		"	
	10.			"	"	1 Man evacuated to F. Amb.	"	
	11.			"	"		"	
	12.			"	"	1 Man rejoined unit from F. Amb.	"	
	13.			"	"		"	
	14.			"	"		"	

LIEUT. R.A.M.C. T.
O.C. 82ND SANITARY SECTION

Army. Form C. 2118.

WAR DIARY
or
INTELLIGENCE SUMMARY.
(Erase heading not required.)

Instructions regarding War Diaries and Intelligence Summaries are contained in F. S. Regs., Part II. and the Staff Manual respectively. Title pages will be prepared in manuscript.

Place	Date	Hour	Summary of Events and Information		Remarks and references to Appendices
			Important orders received	Daily situation	
LOCON.	May 1916 15				Review of Field Works constructed.
	16		Orders received to report on efficiency of C. Solution diluted 20 times.	LOCON and area occupied by 39th Div	Operations in connection with other units in neighbourhood.	Incinerators Latrines Grease traps etc.
	17			"	Sanitary supervision of billets, baths & laundries of divisional area, inspection of water carts, testing of water supplies.	"
	18			"	"	"
	19			"	" Change of Strength.	"
	20			"	"	"
	21			"	"	"
	22			"	"	"
	23			"	" 1 Man evacuated to F. Amb.	"
	24			"	"	"
	25			"	"	"
	26			"	"	"
	27			"	"	"
	28			"	"	"
	29			"	"	"
	30			"	"	"
	31			"	" 1 man evacuated to F. Amb	

Lieut. R.A.M.C. T.
O.C. 82ND SANITARY SECTION

No. 82 San. Section.

June 1916.

82 San/sec
Vol 4

82ND SANITARY SECTION
39TH DIVISION

Army Form C. 2118.

WAR DIARY
or
INTELLIGENCE SUMMARY.
(Erase heading not required.)

Instructions regarding War Diaries and Intelligence Summaries are contained in F. S. Regs., Part II. and the Staff Manual respectively. Title pages will be prepared in manuscript.

Place	Date	Hour	IMPORTANT ORDERS RECEIVED	DAILY SITUATION.	OPERATIONS IN CONNECTION WITH OTHER UNITS IN NEIGHBOURHOOD.	CHANGE OF STRENGTH.	NATURE OF FIELD WORKS CONSTRUCTED	Remarks and references to Appendices
LOCON.	JUNE 1916							
	1	—		Locon and area occupied by 39th Division.	Sanitary supervision of Billets, Baths, laundries of divisional area, inspection & testing of Water Supplies.	1 man rejoined unit from 32nd C.C.S.	Incinerators, latrines, Grease traps, Ablution Benches - etc.	
	2			"	"	1 N.C.O. & man detached for work at La Quesnoy & neighbourhood	"	
	3,4,5,6,7,8,9,10,11			"	"		"	
	12,13,14		Became divisional supply for 'C' Solution.	"	"	4 men reinforcements joined unit.	"	
	15		Issue of 'C' solution commenced	"	"		"	
	16			"	"	1 N.C.O & 1 man detailed for work at V. Chapelle & district. 1 N.C.O & 2 men reinforcement unit from La Quesnoy.	"	
	17			"	"	21st. {1 N.C.O & 1 man detached for work at Richebourg St. V.	"	
	18, 19, 20, 21			"	"		"	
	22			"	"	1 man reinforcement arrived.	"	
	23, 24, 25			"	"		"	
	26			"	"	1 N.C.O. detailed for work duties at Vieille Chapelle.	"	
	27, 28, 29, 30			"	"		"	

O H Miller
LIEUT. R.A.M.C.T.
O/C. 82ND SANITARY SECTION

82ND SANITARY SECTION
39TH. DIVISION

WAR DIARY
or
INTELLIGENCE SUMMARY.
(Erase heading not required.)

Army Form C. 2118.

Instructions regarding War Diaries and Intelligence Summaries are contained in F.S. Regs., Part II. and the Staff Manual respectively. Title pages will be prepared in manuscript.

Place	Date	Hour	Summary of Events and Information			Remarks and references to Appendices
			IMPORTANT ORDERS RECEIVED	DAILY SITUATION	OPERATIONS IN CONNECTION WITH OTHER UNITS IN NEIGHBOURHOOD	CHANGE OF STRENGTH	NATURE OF FIELD WORKS CONSTRUCTED.

Place	Date	Hour	IMPORTANT ORDERS RECEIVED	DAILY SITUATION	OPERATIONS IN CONNECTION WITH OTHER UNITS IN NEIGHBOURHOOD	CHANGE OF STRENGTH	NATURE OF FIELD WORKS CONSTRUCTED.	Remarks
LOCON	JUNE 1916 1	—		LOCON and area occupied by 39th Division	Sanitary Supervision of Billets, Baths, maintenance of divisional area & inspection & testing of Water Supplies.	1 man joined unit from 32nd. C.C.S.	Incinerators, Latrines Grease-Traps, ablution Benches, etc.	
	2			"	"		"	
	3.4.5.6.7.8.9.10.11			"	"	1.N.C.O. & man detailed for work at Le Quesnoy & neighborhood	"	
	12.13.14.			"	"		"	
	15		Became divisional supply for "C" Solution	"	"	4 men reinforcements joined unit	"	
	16.		Issue to "C" Solution commenced.	"	"		"	
	17			"	"	1.N.C.O. 1 man detached for work at V. Chapell echo Fort. 1.N.C.O 1 man reformed work from Le Quesnoy	"	
	18.19.20.21.			"	"	21st { 1.N.C.O 1 man detached for work at Robecq Billiard?	"	
	22.			"	"	1 man Reinforcement arrived	"	
	23.24.25.			"	"		"	
	26			"	"	1.N.C.O. detailed for unit duties at Vieille Chapelle	"	
	27.28.29.30			"	"		"	

C.H.Miller
LIEUT, R.A.M.C. T.
O.C. 82ND SANITARY SECTION

> 82nd
> SANITARY SECTION,
> th DIVISION.
> No. 55/366
> Date 30/6/16

To the D.A.G.
at the Base
Ware Diary for June
enclosed herewith

[signature]
LIEUT. R.A.M.C. (T)
O.C. 82ND SANITARY SECTION

39th Division

82nd. Sanitary Section

July 1916

COMMITTEE FOR THE
MEDICAL HISTORY OF THE WAR
Date 31 AUG. 1915

WAR DIARY or INTELLIGENCE SUMMARY

82ND SANITARY SECTION
39TH DIVISION

Army Form C. 2118.

Place	Date	Hour	IMPORTANT ORDERS RECD.	DAILY SITUATION	OPERATIONS IN CONNECTION WITH OTHER UNITS IN NEIGHBOURHOOD	CHANGE OF STRENGTH	NATURE OF FIELD WORKS CONSTRUCTED.	Remarks and references to Appendices
LOCON	JULY 1916 1			LOCON and area occupied by 39th Div.	Sanitary supervision of Billets, Baths & laundries in Divl area & inspection & testing of water supplies.	1 N.C.O. evacuated to 2d Aust Aux hospital (railway accident) 1 man detailed for work at HQ ADMS via sick convalescent	Incinerators, latrines, grease traps, ablution sheds, Urine Troughs.	
	2			"	"	"	"	
	3.4.5.			"	"	"	"	
	6			"	"	1 reinforcement	"	
	7		Orders recd to move to BETHUNE.	"	"	3 N.C.Os & 2 men detailed latrine repairs.	"	
BETHUNE	8		Moved to BETHUNE & took charge of Bethune & 39th Divisional area.	BETHUNE & 39th Divisional area.	"	1. N.C.O. 1 man " 2 men detailed at Meaphare 1 N.C.O & 1 m. detached for work at BEUVRY.	also Fire pails & latrine paper boxes. Urine Troughs.	
	9			"	"	"	"	
	10. July		Orders that work over to A.D.M.S. 31st Div. Stewart took charge of Bethune from tendering LOCON	"	"	"	"	
	11.12.13			"	"	"	"	
	14.		Orders recd to return to LOCON	"	"	"	"	
LOCON	15.		Returned to LOCON	LOCON etc	"	"	"	
	16			"	"	1. N.C.O & man detached for work at ADS. K. George Rd.	"	
	17			"	"	1. N.C. O. man detached for work at ADMS. H.Qs.	"	
	18.			"	"	1. N.C.O. man returned unit from BEUVRY.	"	

LIEUT. R.A.M.C
O.C. 82ND SANITARY S[ECTION]

82ND SANITARY SECTION
39TH DIVISION

Army Form C. 2118.

WAR DIARY
or
INTELLIGENCE SUMMARY.
(Erase heading not required.)

Instructions regarding War Diaries and Intelligence Summaries are contained in F. S. Regs., Part II. and the Staff Manual respectively. Title pages will be prepared in manuscript.

Place	Date JULY 1916	Hour	IMPORTANT ORDERS RECEIVED	Summary of Events and Information			Remarks and references to Appendices
				DAILY SITUATION	OPERATIONS IN CONNECTION WITH OTHER UNITS IN NEIGHBOURHOOD	CHANGE OF STRENGTH	NATURE OF FIELD WORKS CONSTRUCTED
LOCON	19.20.21.22.23			LOCON + 39th Divl Arr.	Sanitary Supervision of Billets Baths, laundries etc in Divl area & inspection & testing of water supplies		Incinerators, latrines, grease traps, ablution benches, urine troughs etc
	24			"	"	1 N.C.O. now reported unit from K. George Park	"
	25.26.27.28.29.30.31			"	"		"

(2.)

M K Filly
LIEUT. R.A.M.C.T.
O.C. 82ND SANITARY SECTION

(6414) Wt. W3906/P1607 2,500,000 7/18 McA & W Ltd (E 3591) Forms W3091/4.   Army Form W.3091.

Cover for Documents.

Nature of Enclosures.

82 Sanitary Section

my from 1-8-16 — 31-8-16 &
1-9-16 — 30-9-16

Notes, or Letters written.

CONFIDENTIAL
WAR DIARY
OF THE
82nd SANITARY SECTION
R.A.M.C.

From 1st AUGUST 1916   To 31st AUGUST 1916

VOLUME 6

82ND SANITARY SECTION
39TH DIVISION

Instructions regarding War Diaries and Intelligence Summaries are contained in F. S. Regs., Part II. and the Staff Manual respectively. Title pages will be prepared in manuscript.

Army Form C. 2118.

WAR DIARY
or
INTELLIGENCE SUMMARY.
(Erase heading not required.)

Place	Date	Hour	Important orders Received	Daily Situation	Summary of Events and Information — Operations in connection with other units in neighbourhood	Change of Strength	Remarks and references to Appendices — Nature of Field works constructed
	1916 August						
LOCON	1, 2			Locon and 39th Divisional area	Sanitary supervision of Billets Baths and Laundries in Div: area and inspection of water supplies		Incinerators, Latrines, Urinals, Troughs Grease traps, ablution Benches etc.
	3			"	"	3 men attached as a sanitary squad for fatigue duties	"
	4			"	"	2 men attached & returned to A.D.M.S., H.Q.	"
	5, 6, 7, 8			"	"		"
	9			"	"	1 Corpl 3 men detached duties with XI Corps	"
	10			"	"	Rejoined Unit	"
	11		Proceeded St-Michel via LOZINGHEM	"	"		"
LOZINGHEM	12			LOZINGHEM			
ROELLECOURT	13, 14			ROELLECOURT and 39th Divisional area	"		"
	15			"	"	1 N.C.O. & man detached at 134th Field Amb. 2 men detached at 234th Field Co. R.E.	"
	16, 17			"	"		"
	18			"	"	11 T.U. men attached for Sanitary fatigue duties	"
	19, 20, 21			"	(L.)		"

Capt R.A.M.C., T.
O.C. 82ND SANITARY SECTION

82nd SANITARY SECTION
39TH. DIVIS C.N

Army Form C. 2118.

WAR DIARY
or
INTELLIGENCE SUMMARY.
(Erase heading not required.)

Instructions regarding War Diaries and Intelligence Summaries are contained in F.S. Regs., Part II. and the Staff Manual respectively. Title pages will be prepared in manuscript.

Place	Date	Hour	Important Orders Received	Daily Situation	Summary of Events and Information		Remarks and references to Appendices
					Operations in connection with other units in neighbourhood	Change of strength	Nature of Field Works constructed
	1916 August						
ROELLECOURT	22		Orders to proceed to HONVAL on 23rd	ROELLECOURT	Sanitary supervision of billets, baths, laundries in Divisional area and inspection of water supplies	1 NCO and 3 men on detached duties re-joined unit	
	23		To proceed to LE SUISSE on 24th	HONVAL			
	24		To proceed to Sans St LEGER instead of LE SUISSE. To proceed on 25th to BOIS DE WARNIMONT	SUS ST. LEGER			
	25			BOIS DE WARNIMONT	During halt at—water bottles of some hundreds of filled the K.R.R.		
	26			"	—		
	27		To proceed on 28th to ACHEUX		—	1 NCO and 1 man detached for work under Town Major, ENGLEBELMER	
	28			ACHEUX and 39th Divisional area	—		
	29			"	Sanitary supervision of billets, camps, baths and laundries in Divisional Area and inspection of water supplies		
	30				15 NCOs and men carried out Sanitary work at the V Corps Collecting Station	15 NCOs and men carried out Sanitary work at the V Corps Collecting Station	
	31						

[signature] Capt.
O.C. 82ND SANITARY SECTION

CONFIDENTIAL

WAR DIARY

OF THE

82ND SANITARY SECTION

R.A.M.C.

From 1st SEPTEMBER 1916 to 30th SEPTEMBER 1916.

VOLUME 7

82nd SANITARY SECTION
39TH. DIVISION

Army Form C. 2118.

WAR DIARY
or
INTELLIGENCE SUMMARY.
(Erase heading not required.)

Instructions regarding War Diaries and Intelligence Summaries are contained in F. S. Regs., Part II. and the Staff Manual respectively. Title pages will be prepared in manuscript.

Place	Date	Hour	IMPORTANT ORDERS RECIEVED	DAILY SITUATION	OPERATIONS IN CONNECTION WITH OTHER UNITS IN NEIGHBOURHOOD	CHANGE OF STRENGTH	NATURE OF FIELD WORKS CONSTRUCTED	Remarks and references to Appendices
ACHEUX	SEPT. 1916. 1			ACHEUX & 39th Divl area	Sanitary Supervision Plunger Rolls Baths reinstated in Bath and inspection of water supplies.		Incinerators, latrines, urine troughs, grease traps, ablution benches, meat safes, etc.	
	2			"	15 N.C.O's army carried out sanitary works at new V Corps Collecting Stn.		"	
	3, 4.			"	21 N.C.O's army assisted 134 Fd Amb in evacuation of wounded at 61/55 Col. Stn. The Stretcher bearers, fitted with special movable seats		"	
	5.			"	transported sitting cases to Corps C.S. Sanitary Supervision of Divisional area	1. N.C.O 1 man detached for work at HOUVENCOURT. 1. N.C.O detached for work at BEAUSSART.	"	
	6, 7, 8, 9.			"			"	
	10.			"		1 man detached BEAUSSART. N.C.O 2 men MAILLY-MAILLET	"	
	11, 12, 13, 14.			"	11. N.C.O's 4 men assisted 134th Fd Amb in evacuation of wounded at Corps Col. Stn		"	
	15			"	10. N.C.O's 4 men — do —		"	
	16			"	Sanitary Supervision of Divisional area		"	
	17, 18, 19, 20, 21, 22, 23, 24, 25			"	11. N.C.O. 1 man assisted 134th Fd Amb at Corps Collecting Station		"	
	26, 27, 28			"	Motor Lorry for ransport of burial party 133 Fd Amb to New Cal. Stn 26 9pm-3 am		"	
	27, 29, 30			"	Sanitary Supervision of Divisional area		"	

> 82nd
> SANITARY SECTION,
> th DIVISION.
> No. SS/1378
> Date 7.1.17

A.D.M.S.
 39th Div.

Duplicate copy of War Diary for September 1916 is now forwarded for transmission to O. i/c Records, please.

C. H. Lilley.
Capt. R.A.M.C.T.
O.C. 82ND SANITARY SECTION

CONFIDENTIAL Vol 7

140/1949

Duplicate Oct.1916

WAR DIARY
OF THE
82nd SANITARY SECTION.
R.A.M.C.T.

From 1st OCTOBER 1916 to 31st OCTOBER 1916

VOLUME 8.

COMMITTEE FOR THE
MEDICAL HISTORY OF THE WAR
Date 30 APR.1917

82nd SANITARY SECTION
39TH DIVISION

Army Form C. 2118.

WAR DIARY
or
INTELLIGENCE SUMMARY.
(Erase heading not required.)

Place	Date	Hour	IMPORTANT ORDERS RECEIVED	DAILY SITUATION	OPERATIONS IN CONNECTION WITH OTHER UNITS IN NEIGHBOURHOOD	CHANGE OF STRENGTH	NATURE OF FIELD WORKS CONSTRUCTED	Remarks and references to Appendices
ACHEUX	OCT. 1916 1			ACHEUX & 39th 2nd aux	Sanitary supervision of camps Billets, baths, including inspection of water supplies		Incinerators, latrines, troughs, grease traps, ablution benches, meat safes &c.	
	2.3.4			"	"	4. N.C.O.'s & men rejoined on completion of detached duties		
ENGLEBELMER	5		Instruction recd to move H.Q. to ENGLEBELMER on 5.10.16					
	6			ENGLEBELMER	"	1. N.C.O. man detached MARTINSART	"	N.C.O. at LANCASHIRE DUMP returned. 1 RANGE turnip road for installing services prior to construction on road
	7			"	"	1. N.C.O. attd for works duties at LANCASHIRE DUMP	"	
	8.9.10.11			"	"	[illegible]	"	
	12		Orders recd to move to D.H.Q. Camp on 13.10.16	"	"	1. N.C.O. detached for duties at Reserve Army H.Q.	"	
BOUZINCOURT	13			BOUZINCOURT CAMP	"		"	
	14.15.16.17.18.19			"	"		"	
	20			"	"	1. N.C.O. & men rejoined unit from MARTINSART	"	
	21.22.23.24.25			"	"		"	
	26			"	"	N.C.O. returned for work at II Corps. H.Q.	"	
	27.28.29.30.31			"	"		"	

Capt. R.A.M.C.

14d/862

39th Div.

82nd Sanitary Section

Nov. 1916

COMMITTEE FOR THE
MEDICAL HISTORY OF THE WAR
Date −3 JAN. 1917

CONFIDENTIAL WAR DIARY

of the

82ND SANITARY SECTION

R.A.M.C.T.

From 1st NOVEMBER 1916 to 30th NOVEMBER 1916.

VOLUME 9

Army Form C. 2118.

WAR DIARY
or
INTELLIGENCE SUMMARY.
(Erase heading not required).

Instructions regarding War Diaries and Intelligence Summaries are contained in F. S. Regs., Part II. and the Staff Manual respectively. Title pages will be prepared in manuscript.

Place	Date	Hour	Summary of Events and Information	Remarks and references to Appendices
BOUZINCOURT.	Nov. 1916			
	1	10 a.m.	Visited billets in SENLIS occupied by this Division; drew attention of ADMS to system of pits in this area.	
	2	10 a.m.	Made a round of HQ Sanitation and found same in a satisfactory condition.	
	3	9 a.m.	Visited River ANCRE with reference to notices relating to water supplies & reported on same.	
	4	2 p.m.	Drew attention of ADMS to excessive speed & unloading of a water-cart of this Division.	
	4	2 p.m.	Interviewed Town Major of SENLIS with reference to use of Baths there, and found that these were, on notice being given, available for this Division.	
	5	10 a.m.	Routine inspection – MARTINSART village	
	6	10 a.m.	" – Artillery billets etc.	
	7	10 a.m.	Visited 227th Coy R.E. re position of ablution benches on Pioneer Rd.	
	8	–	With permission of ADMS did not go out on duties.	
	9	–	Selected site along with N.C.O.s R.E. for new Ablution benches on Pioneer Rd. Inspection of Billets on Pioneer Road.	
	10	10 a.m.	Visited AUTHUILLE & selected a site for Public Latrine.	
	11	10 a.m.	Visited AMIENS to obtain certain tools necessary for structural work.	
	12		Warned to be ready to proceed to LANCASHIRE DUMP Aid Post for duty	

T2134. Wt. W708–776. 500000. 4/15. Sir J. C. & S.

Army Form C. 2118.

WAR DIARY
or
INTELLIGENCE SUMMARY.
(Erase heading not required.)

Instructions regarding War Diaries and Intelligence Summaries are contained in F. S. Regs., Part II. and the Staff Manual respectively. Title pages will be prepared in manuscript.

Place	Date	Hour	Summary of Events and Information	Remarks and references to Appendices
BOUZINCOURT	Nov 1916 13	5 am	Reported for duty to O.C. 132nd Fd. Amb. Assisted in dressing wounded who began to arrive 7.30 am. Kept fully occupied till 4 pm. Took night duty 1 am – 4 am.	
	14	10 am	Reported at Aid Post COOKERS for duty – withdrawn 2 hrs later on orders of A.D.M.S and returned in car with him to BOUZINCOURT	
	15	9.30 am	Received orders to be ready to move out; section lorry packed; camp cleared	
	16	7.30 am	Section moved out 7.30 am; lorry moved out 9 am.	
BEAUVAL		4.30 pm	Section arrived BEAUVAL	
	17	–	Section remained at BEAUVAL	
	18	1 pm	Section marched to CANDAS	
		3 pm	Section arrived at "	
		8 pm	Section entrained at "	
ESQUELBECQ	19	4 am	Section arrived at ESQUELBECQ.	
	20	–	Visited parts of 118th Inf. Bde. area	
	21	–	Visited parts of 117th Inf. Bde area.	
	22	–	Visited K & L Camps.	
	23	–	Office work – arranging detached parties.	

R. H. Pillay
Capt. R.A.M.C.
O.C. 52nd Sanitary Section

Army Form C. 2118.

WAR DIARY
or
INTELLIGENCE SUMMARY.
(Erase heading not required.)

Instructions regarding War Diaries and Intelligence Summaries are contained in F. S. Regs., Part II. and the Staff Manual respectively. Title pages will be prepared in manuscript.

Place	Date	Hour	Summary of Events and Information	Remarks and references to Appendices
ESQUELBECQ	Nov 1916. 24	9 am	Inspected K.L.M & Y camps along with A.D.M.S and made recommendations	
	25	9 am	" 118th Brigade area "	
	26	9.45 am	" 117th "	
	27	9 am	Div. H.Q. ESQUELBECQ	
		2 pm	To A.D.M.S at WORMHOUDT re detached party	
	28	9 am	Inspected Baths at BOLLEZEELE, WORMHOUDT and Laundry WORMHOUDT.	
	29	9 am	Interviewed M.O's 13th Gloucesters and 16 R.B.'s re Water Supply and Latrines and advised	
		2 pm	" O.C. 9th Pontoon Park re supply of empty oil tins for sanitary purposes	
	30	9 am	Inspected billets recently vacated by 4/5 Black Watch.	
		2 pm	" water pumping plant at WORMHOUDT.	

82nd SANITARY SECTION, 39th DIVISION.
No. SS/1110
Date 30·11·1916

A.D.M.S.
39th Div.

Enclosed is War Diary of this Section for November, 1916.

C H Lilley
Capt., R.A.M.C. T.
O.C. 82ND SANITARY SECTION

CONFIDENTIAL

39th Div.
14/909.
Vol 10

Dec 1916

WAR DIARY
OF THE
82nd SANITARY SECTION
R.A.M.C.T

FROM 1st DECEMBER 1916 to 31st DECEMBER 1916

VOLUME 10.

COMMITTEE FOR THE
MEDICAL HISTORY OF
Date

Army Form C. 2118.

WAR DIARY
or
INTELLIGENCE SUMMARY
(Erase heading not required.)

Instructions regarding War Diaries and Intelligence Summaries are contained in F.S. Regs., Part II. and the Staff Manual respectively. Title pages will be prepared in manuscript.

Place	Date	Hour	Summary of Events and Information	Remarks and references to Appendices
ESQUELBECQ	Dec 1916 1	9. am	Inspected Y & K camps and formulated reports to A.D.M.S.; also inspected Tank No 30 & its source of supply.	
		2.15 pm	Interviewed Sanitary Officer 38th Division re detached party of this section to be under his supervision while a Brigade of this Division are in the line	
	2	9. am	Writing reports & other routine Office work. Interviewed Porton Park re possibility of supplying this unit with oil-drums, etc.	
		2. pm		
	3	9.30 am	Sunday Parade Service; drafted order re units supplying the section with horses &/or conversion into Sanitary articles.	
		2 pm	Inspected sanitary arrangements at all Div. H.Q. Units	
	4	9. am	Inspected 126 Bde billets etc., along with M.O. Met water cart of 184 Bde B. Batt. and inspected it & subsequently met the O/C & advised it to be sent to workshop for thorough overhaul — this has been done.	
		2 pm.	Preparation of Water Report re supplies in Divisional Area	
	5	9. am	Received order to deliver a lecture on Sanitation on the March, in Camps & Billets at Divisional Schools, VOLKERINCKHOVE. Day occupied in preparation.	
	6	9 am	Reinspected Divisional Hq. Three men detached for duty in the ARNEKE area.	

Army Form C. 2118.

WAR DIARY
or
INTELLIGENCE SUMMARY.
(Erase heading not required.)

Instructions regarding War Diaries and Intelligence Summaries are contained in F. S. Regs., Part II. and the Staff Manual respectively. Title pages will be prepared in manuscript.

Place	Date	Hour	Summary of Events and Information	Remarks and references to Appendices
	Dec 1916			
ESQUELBECQ	6	6pm	Delivered lecture as above at Divisional Schools, VOLKERINCKHOVE.	
	7	9am	Attended at A.D.M.S. office to interview O.C. 38th Divisional San. Sec and later went round part of the area with him	
		2pm	Inspected new Drying Room WORMHOUDT.	
	8th	9am	Completed inspection of Artillery units with M.O. 186 Bde. R.F.A. at	
	9th	9am	Inspected late billets of 13th & rest at ZEGERS-CAPPEL & found same had been left clean " billets 16.R.B. at BOLLEZEELE.	
	10th	9.30am	Sunday Parade.	
		2pm	Routine Office Work.	
	11	9.am	Accompanied A.D.M.S. in a visit to his area. A.D.M.S. inspected outgoing Sanitary Section's billets & approved of them being taken over by 82nd Sanitary Sect.	
		2pm	Visited P.J.E. camps and Canal bank along with O.C. 38th Div Sanitary Section	
	12	9am	Advance party of 82nd Sanitary Section :- 1 N.C.O. & 2 men took over from 38th Div. San. Sec.	
		2pm	Detached party at BOLLEZEELE returned.	
	13	9am	Made a trial inspection of Div. H.Q. & found same in a clean condition. Advance party of 38th Div. San. Sec. arrived.	

T2134. Wt. W708—776. 500000. 4/15. Sir J. C. & S.

WAR DIARY
or
INTELLIGENCE SUMMARY.
(Erase heading not required.)

Army Form C. 2118.

Instructions regarding War Diaries and Intelligence Summaries are contained in F. S. Regs., Part II. and the Staff Manual respectively. Title pages will be prepared in manuscript.

Place	Date	Hour	Summary of Events and Information	Remarks and references to Appendices
PESELHOEK	Dec 1916 14	9 am	Whole section moved to new location A 14 d 50 (Sheet 2e)	
	15	9 am	Interviewed A.D.M.S at H.Q. re inspection of area, detachment of parties, etc.	
	16	9 am	Inspected Div. H.Q. Found large accumulation of refuse around incinerator. An N.C.O. and man were, with the approval of the A.D.M.S. detached for work at each of the following places:— Divisional H.Q., 134 Fd. Amb. A.D.S (East farm) and E Camp.	
	17	9 am	Inspected the area lately occupied by the French and reported condition of same to A.D.M.S. and made necessary recommendations.	
	18	9 am	Inspected S camp	
		2 pm	Inspected P camp	
	19	9 am	Inspected Canal Bank Interviewed Brigade Major 116th Bde and Canal Bank Adjutant re various points connected with the Sanitation.	
		2 pm	Called at A.D.M.S. Office	
	20	9 am	Inspected J Camp	
		2 pm	Office work	
	21	9 am	Inspected D Camp	
		11 am	Inspected E Camp	

R.K. Lilley Capt.

WAR DIARY
or
INTELLIGENCE SUMMARY.
(Erase heading not required.)

Army Form C. 2118.

Place	Date	Hour	Summary of Events and Information	Remarks and references to Appendices
PESELHOEK	Dec 1916 21	10.30am	Received orders to attend at Senior Officers' School at 10.am 22nd Dec to explain and demonstrate the water cart.	
	22	10.0am	Attended at Senior Officers' School and reported to Camp Adjutant. Was not called upon to demonstrate the water cart.	
		2pm	Reported at A.D.M.S. Office.	
	23	9am	Along with Railhead Supply Officer inspected the sanitation at Railhead. Made recommendations & offered assistance in carrying these out.	
		2pm	Office Work.	
	24	9am	Reinspected Baths at A14.b.54, found a new N.C.O. in charge from 132nd Fd. Amb., and that a purer effluent was being obtained than hitherto. instructed N.C.O. in the precipitation — sedimentation processes. Inspected two water-carts on way to J Camp I found them in good condition.	
		2.30pm	Attended conference at A.D.M.S. Office. Chief topics were :— i. War diaries ii. Ventilation & lighting in huts iii. The necessity for training of newly joined officers & for opportunities of discussion amongst the R.A.M.C. Officers of the Division.	

C.H. Tilley
Major R.A.M.C.
O.C. 52ND SANITARY SECTION

Army Form C. 2118.

WAR DIARY
or
INTELLIGENCE SUMMARY.
(Erase heading not required.)

Place	Date	Hour	Summary of Events and Information	Remarks and references to Appendices
PESELHOEK	Dec 1916 25		Christmas Day.	
		5 pm	Conveyed A.D.M.S.' Christmas & New Year Greetings to the Section.	
		4.15 pm	Received orders to attend at D.D.M.S Office (VIII Corps) at 10. am on 26th Dec.	
	26	10 am	Attended at Office of D.D.M.S. VIII Corps. Conference which was to have been with regard to the institution of a School of Sanitation for Sanitary Orderlies was postponed on account of absence of two other Sanitary Officers. D.D.M.S. made various inquiries re sanitation in 39th Divisional area, methods of working etc.	
	27	9 am	Inspected G. Camp.	
		2 pm	Re-inspected P Camp	
	28th	9 am	Inspected wagon-lines of Divisional Artillery along with M.O. (Capt Craven)	
		3 pm	Office Work.	
	29	9 am	Inspected all sections of D.A.C. along with M.O. (Capt Ferguson)	
	30	9 am	Inspected J camp, found same about to be occupied as a school of instruction by 38th Division: also considerable improvements in hand.	
	31	9 am	Office Work; formulating weekly Sanitary Report & transcribing War Diary.	

C K Millar
O 62nd SANITARY SECTION R.A.M.C. T.

Army Form C. 2118.

WAR DIARY
or
INTELLIGENCE SUMMARY.
(Erase heading not required.)

Instructions regarding War Diaries and Intelligence Summaries are contained in F.S. Regs., Part II. and the Staff Manual respectively. Title pages will be prepared in manuscript.

Place	Date	Hour	Summary of Events and Information	Remarks and references to Appendices
PESELHOEK	Dec 1916 31	cntd.	Inspection F camp (about to be occupied as a school of Musketry) along with Capt Mills M.O. Suggested that as the necessary ground was available urine should be disposed of by sprinkling on land: the area to be divided into seven parts - one to be used each day thus permitting 6 days rest to each area. Capt Mills agreed to make observations in this system & to report any signs of a nuisance arising.	

R.H. Lilley
Capt. R.A.M.C. T.
O.C. 92ND SANITARY SECTION

> 82nd
> SANITARY SECTION.
> th DIVISION.
> No. SS/1379
> Date. 1.1.17

A.D.M.S.
39th Div.

Enclosed is War Diary of this Section for December 1916 with appropriate cover, please

C. H. Lilley
Capt. R.A.M.C. T.
O.C. 82ND SANITARY SECTION

39

140/943

Vol XI

Confidential

39th Div

Jan. 1917

War Diary
of the
82nd Sanitary Section
R.A.M.C.

From 1st January 1917 to 31st January 1917.

Volume II.

COMMITTEE FOR THE
MEDICAL HISTORY OF THE WAR
Date   13 MAR. 1917

Original

# Army Form C. 2118.

82ND SANITARY SECTION
WAR DIARY or INTELLIGENCE SUMMARY

(Erase heading not required.)

I

Place	Date	Hour	Summary of Events and Information	Remarks and references to Appendices
PESELHOEK	Jan. 1917 1		At request of O/C conferred and advised as to Water Supply at 134th Field Ambulance.	
	2		Made a general inspection of the whole of the Canal Bank with Senior M.O.	
			Inspections at ELVERDINGHE. At A.D.M.S. Office made responsible for Divisional weekly Sanitary Report.	
	3		Office Routine. Preparation for Lecture. Conference of Regimental M.O.'s, at 134th Field Ambulance. Correspondence etc.	
	4		Inspection of "P" and "F" Camps with Camp Adjutant.	
	5		Inspection of A.S.C. Nos. 1, 2, 3 and 4 Coys, at PROVEN. Visited Field Cashier and O.C. 55th Aust. Sanitary Section.	
	6		Office routine and weekly Sanitary Report.	
	7		Conference with Town Sanitary Officer POPERINGHE re Lectures. Interviewed A.D.M.S. re new area.	
	8		Interviewed Camp Adjt. re P and F Camps. Demonstrated use of Water Cart to M.O., O.C., and Adjutant. Advised cart be sent to workshop for necessary overhauling and repairs.	
	9		Visited O.C. 134 Fd. Amb. to obtain a N.C.O. Instructor for School.	
	10		Conferred with O/C 55 Fld. Sanitary Section. Inspected 9 B, C and O Camps.	
	11		Attended lecture at POPERINGHE and conference at A.D.M.S. Office.	
	12		Conferred with O/c 55 Divl. Sanitary Section.	
	13		Attended conference at Officers' Club POPERINGHE re School of Sanitation.	
	14		Attended R.M.S. Office re reference to weekly report, disinfection of blankets and School of Sanitation — models and diagrams.	
	15		Moved to the Laiterie, POPERINGHE. Delivered lecture at School of Sanitation. Interviewed Town Mayor of POPERINGHE.	

WAR DIARY / INTELLIGENCE SUMMARY

Army Form C. 2118.
82ND SANITARY SECTION

Place	Date	Hour	Summary of Events and Information	Remarks and references to Appendices
POPERINGHE	JAN. 1917. 16	morn.	Re-inspected "A", "B", "C" and "O" Camps.	
	17	aftn.	Delivered Lecture at "School".	
	18		Inspected Baths at POPERINGHE. Visited YPRES. Interviewed M.O. i/c 39 D.S., Town Major, Staff Captain 116th and 118th Brigades. Inspected Baths which were not working.	
	19		Lectured at "School". Attended A.D.M.S. Office. Conferred with M.O. i/c Skin H. and advised as to treatment of ablution water, grease trap, latrines &c.	
	20		Attended A.D.M.S. Office re "Health Report". Compiled weekly Sanitary report. Tested two men detailed to work horse-drawn (Barclay & Perkins) disinfector.	
	21		Inspected Divisional Dumps. Attended A.D.M.S Office, Corps H.Q., and 134th Field Amb.	
	22		Lectured at "School". Visited HAZEBROUCK.	
	23		Re-inspected Camps "C", "O" and "B".	
	24		Delivered Lecture at School.	
	25		General re-inspection of YPRES area. Conferred with Town Major.	
	26	morn.	Capt. C. H. LILLEY O/c 82nd Sanitary Section unit arrived and evacuated to C.C.S. Work carried on by Staff Sergeant under supervision of A.D.M.S.	
	28		Capt. Robertson, D.D. R.A.M.C. took over temporary command of Unit.	
	29		Attended Conference at Army School Sanitation HAZEBROUCK re standardising all sanitary structures to suit its division arrived at.	
	29.		Weather very cold. Inspection work being carried on — Lectured at Corps School Sanitation POPERINGHE 2–4 p.m. on Camp Sanitation — latrines — urinals —.	
	30		"Very frosty & cold" —	
	31.		Reported sick to 173 Fd Ambulance — work being carried on satisfactorily.	

G.M. Robertson
Capt. R.A.M.C.
O.C. 82ND SANITARY SECTION.

Feb. 1917
39th Div.
140/1994
Vol 12

Confidential

War Diary
of the
82nd Sanitary Section,
R.A.M.C. (T.)

From 1st February 1917 to 28th February 1917.

VOLUME 12

COMMITTEE FOR THE
MEDICAL HISTORY OF THE WAR
Date 4.- APR. 1917

A.D.M.S.
39th Division
___

With reference to the
attached War Diary, on
taking over the section
I could find no trace
of previous entries for
the month of February.
It is therefore presumed
that Capt. ROBERTSON
R.A.M.C, who was in
command prior to
myself has taken
the Diary with him.
He was evacuated
sick.

J.A. Porter Capt.
R A M C
1/3/17   O.C 62nd Sanitry S[ec]

Army Form C. 2118.

Tel: Number 1
Intelligence No 1
82ND SANITARY SECTION

WAR DIARY
or
INTELLIGENCE SUMMARY

(Erase heading not required.)

Instructions regarding War Diaries and Intelligence
Summaries are contained in F.S. Regs., Part II.
and the Staff Manual respectively. Title Pages
will be prepared in manuscript.

Place	Date	Hour	Summary of Events and Information	Remarks and references to Appendices
Esquelbecq	Feby 19th	—	Capt. J.H. PORTER R.A.M.C. appointed temporary OC No 82 Sanitary Section as a temporary measure, pending arrival of Officer detailed for this charge. Visited 116 Infantry Brigade Area at BOLLEZEELE. Sanitation very primitive. Report rendered to ADMS 39th Division	J.P. Porter
"	20		Visited Nos. 133 and 134 Fd. Ambs. with ADMS, thence to PROVEN. Sen 1350 francs for payment of Section. Detailed Inspection of 116 Infantry Brigade at BOLLEZEELE made in afternoon, and report rendered. Men paid.	JHP
"	21		Visited RENINGHELST with DADMS & Saw 23rd Division Headquarters & OC No 40 Sanitary Section from whom this section will take over, at WARATAH CAMP. Later in day, calciaphates Carridina	JHP
"	22		Visited 117 Infantry Brigade Area with ADMS and Lt/Col STEWART. HQ RAMC 39th Division. Received orders regarding forthcoming move. Section to move to WARATAH CAMP on 26th inst., advance party to proceed on 25th February. Consisting of advp to detached parties etc	JHP
"	23		Arrears of office work cleared up & arrangements for move proceeding.	JHP
"	24		Routine. Office work & arrangements being made for move.	JHP

Army Form C. 2118.

WAR DIARY
or
INTELLIGENCE SUMMARY

(Erase heading not required.)

82nd SANITARY SECTION

Instructions regarding War Diaries and Intelligence Summaries are contained in F.S. Regs., Part II. and the Staff Manual respectively. Title Pages will be prepared in manuscript.

Place	Date	Hour	Summary of Events and Information	Remarks and references to Appendices
Esquelbecq	Feby 25	—	Section Sany. intr advance party preceded WARATAH CAMP at 9.30 am. Report on Sanitation of area rendered to A.D.M.S. Arrangements for tomorrow's move to habitation of personnel being made. Carpenter sent to RENINGHELST to arrange hut there.	JHP
"	26th	—	Packing up. Section move to new site at 11.30 am Ration G.S. picked up at HERTZEELE. Lorry to return on 27th inst. for extra equipment stores.	JHP
"	27'	—	Section arrived at WARATAH CAMP & took over from No 40 Sanitary Section & yesterday. Detachments as hitherto. as follows: Camp Adj. Commandant 1 NCO Corps Headquarters 1 NCO Corps School of Sanitation 1 NCO YPRES 1 NCO. 1 man Inspection for various areas detailed & arrangements.	JHP
"	28th	—	Prepared monthly Sanitary Report required by X Corps 7 rendered same to A.D.M.S. Report on Bath water in YPRES received, action taken.	JHP

JHPorter Capt
R.A.M.C.
O.C. 82ND SANITARY SECTION

2449 Wt. W14957/M90 750,000 1/16 J.B.C. & A. Forms/C.2118/12.

CONFIDENTIAL

39th Div.

WAR DIARY
OF THE
82nd SANITARY SECTION
R.A.M.C.(T.)

From 1st March 1917 to 31st March 1917

VOLUME 3

COMMITTEE FOR THE
MEDICAL HISTORY OF THE WAR
Date 11 MAY. 1917

Army Form C. 2118.

WAR DIARY
or
INTELLIGENCE SUMMARY.
(Erase heading not required.)

82ND SANITARY SECTION

Place	Date	Hour	Summary of Events and Information	Remarks and references to Appendices
WARATAH CAMP T.15.a.6.9 (Sheet 28)	March 4		Took over charge of Section from Capt. M. Porter R.A.M.C. Office work.	
	5		Conferred with D.A.D.M.S. on taking over the Section. Inspected No 2 Section D.A.C. Camp and Sanitary Section Camp. Visited Foden disinfector and Water Tanks No 6, and 32. Selected site for new hut for Sanitary Section Office.	
	6		Accompanied A.D.M.S. on tour of inspection of the Sanitary Section Camp. Inspected Toronto, and Montreal Camps. Arranged with proprietor of land for removal of Sanitary Section Camp to new site adjacent to road.	
	7		Interviewed D.A.D.M.S. on rendering of reports, and removal of camp. Inspected Divisional Theatre Camp and reported. D.A.D.M.S. Attended conference at Hamerlinghe at 2.30 p.m. Reports and other office work.	
	8		Drew money from Field Cashier for payment of Section. Office work. Inspected Camps of Mob. Vety. Section, and D.A.D.O.S.	
	9		Office routine. Paid Section. Attended lecture at Corps H.Q. on Sanitation	
	10		Visited A.D.M.S. Inspected, and reported on Wyomyng Camp. Inspected St Laurence and Erie Camps. Reports and Office work	
	11		Office work. Made inspection with Capt de Grent R.A.M.C. of trench	

Constant Ponder Capt R.A.M.C.
O.C. 22ND SANITARY SECTION

Army Form C. 2118.

WAR DIARY
or
INTELLIGENCE SUMMARY
(Erase heading not required.)

82ND SANITARY SECTION

Instructions regarding War Diaries and Intelligence Summaries are contained in F. S. Regs., Part II. and the Staff Manual respectively. Title pages will be prepared in manuscript.

Place	Date	Hour	Summary of Events and Information	Remarks and references to Appendices
WARATAH CAMP G.15.a.6.9	12		system occupied by Right Battalion. Left side Office work. Inspected source of polluted water used by 13th Gloster Transport, and reported on same	
	13		Office work. Inspected whole of right side centre section of front line	
	14		Visited A.D.M.S. and made further reports. Office routine	
	15		Office routine. Inspected trench system occupied by Left Battalion of Left side	
	16		Inspected Infantry Barracks Ypres and surroundings. Office routine.	
	17		Office routine. Armstrong Hut moved to new site near road. Moved from hut in Waratah Camp to latter.	
G.15.a.7.8	18		Office hut removed to new position near road. Office routine	
	19		Office routine. Men's sleeping hut taken down	
	20		Office routine. Men's sleeping hut re-erected on new site	
	21		Office routine	
	22		Drew money from Field Cashier. Office routine.	
	23		Inspected Divisional Train Nos 1, 2 and 3 Coys. Paid Section. Office routine.	

Graham Parker Capt R.A.M.C. T.
O.C. 82ND SANITARY SECTION

Army Form C. 2118.

WAR DIARY
or
INTELLIGENCE SUMMARY
(Erase heading not required.)

82ND SANITARY SECTION

Place	Date	Hour	Summary of Events and Information	Remarks and references to Appendices
WARATAH CAMP G.15.a.7/2.	24		Office routine. Inspected D.A.C. Nos 1 and 3 Sections	
	25		Visited A.D.M.S Office. Inspected proposed H.Q Camp, and surveyed same for provision of extra accomodation. Office routine. Visited Canadian Construction Coy re Water Supply. Inspected new public latrine near Prisoners cage. Visited A.D.M.S. Office.	
	26		Office routine and reports	
	27		Office routine. Inspected 126th Heavy Battery	
	28		Visited Foden Disinfecting Station. Office routine.	
	29		Office routine and Returns for S.S. Mos of Sanitation constructions issued during March	
	30		Office routine. Inspected 194th Brigade R.F.A. Waggon Lines and all Batteries	
	31		Office routine. Inspected 184th Brigade R.F.A. Waggon Lines and all Batteries	

Constant Ponder Capt.
O.C. 22ND SANITARY SECTION

Appendix No. 1

S.S./R.87

A.D.M.S.

39th. Division.

MONTHLY SANITARY REPORT ON AREA OCCUPIED BY 39th. DIV.

The 83nd. Sanitary Section moved into the Xth. Corps area on 26th. February, 1917, and detachments have been posted as follows -
- Xth. Corps Headquarters . . . . 1 N.C.O.
- Xth. Corps School of Sanitation . . 1 N.C.O.
- Area Commandant, ABEELE . . . . . . 1 N.C.O.
- YPRES . . . . 1 N.C.O. and 1 man.

The condition of the area on taking over was generally fair, but in many instances especially at the Headquarters Camp, RENING-HELST, much rubbish was left undisposed of.

In the two days at our disposal, it has not been possible to make a detailed inspection of the whole area, but the following is a general survey of the conditions which are in existence and of proposed improvements :-

1. BILLETS - On the whole are in good repair and clean. Attention should be given to light and ventilation. Night urine pails are required in places.

2. COOKHOUSES - Field kitchens are used by most Formations. Flooring requires attention and should if possible be bricked. Grease traps are generally dirty and require cleansing and renewal of filtering medium. Attention should be directed to orders regarding the covering of food and meat safes. It is strongly urged that cooks and their assistants be provided with washable clothing, as being more sanitary and as the sight of a dirty and greasy cook is not conducive to a healthy appetite.

3. ABLUTION. Benches are provided but not in sufficient quantity. It is recommended that brick flooring or trench board stands be made where these do not already exist. In some cases the soapy water is not properly filtered, and the Soap Hopper filter box should in these instances be obtained.

4. CONSERVANCY.- The fly proof box system with pails predominates, and is in fairly good condition. Flooring of Latrines and approaches thereto with bricks or duck-boards should be carried out. Faeces are incinerated and this would be greatly facilitated were a larger supply of saw-dust obtainable for use in latrines.

5. INCINERATORS.- Generally in good condition and working effectively. Many accumulations of unburnt refuse have been left by the out-going Units, but this is now being satisfactorily disposed of. It is recommended that small covered platforms of brick or cement be erected near incinerators for the dumping and mixing of refuse.

6. DRAINAGE. This is good, being greatly facilitated by the configuration of the ground in this area.

(Signed)

J.H. PORTER
Capt., R.A.M.C.
O.C. 83nd. Sanitary Section.

March 1st. 1917.

(4) WO95/2579

50 Mobile Veterinary Section

Mar 1916 — Jan 1919

39TH DIVISION

50TH MOBILE VETY SECN

MAR 1916 - JAN 1919

SO M Vetter

Vol 1

Mar '16
Jan '19

Army Form C. 2118.

WAR DIARY
or
INTELLIGENCE SUMMARY

(Erase heading not required.)

50th Mobile Vety Section
39th Division

Instructions regarding War Diaries and Intelligence Summaries are contained in F. S. Regs, Part II. and the Staff Manual respectively. Title Pages will be prepared in manuscript.

Place	Date	Hour	Summary of Events and Information	Remarks and references to Appendices
Left Witley	4-3-16	3 A.M.	Left Godalming Siding 6.15 A.M. en route for Southampton	
Southampton	4-3-16	9.15 A.M	Embarked Southampton 10 A.M. The Hunts craft sailed from Southampton 8 P.m.	
Arrived Havre	8-3-16		Disembarked Havre, proceeded to Dock Rest Camp	
Left Havre	9-3-16		Entrained Havre for Steenbecque	
Arrived Steenbecque	10-3-16		Quartered at Farm	
	12-3-16		Collected horses from various farms left by 23rd Divn.	
	14-3-16		Evacuated 10 horses to 13th Vety Hospl. Neuf Chatel.	
	19-3-16		Pay to men 2·30 frs	
	19-3-16		Collected 3 bad foot cases belonging to 184th Bde R.F.A.	
	22-3-16		Received 10 H.D. horses from 53rd D.A.C. 6 of which were suffering from Laminitis	
	23-3-16		Evac 24 horses 2 mules to 13th Vety Hospl. Neuf Chatel.	
	26-3-16		Collected 18 horses 4 mules from 28·4th Divn A.S.C. These were surplus horses due to amalgamation of 4·2·S·s· Black Watch, nearly all in bad condition, debilitated, and covered with lice through neglect, few were lame	
	27-3-16		Evac 24 horses to 13th Vety Hospl. Neuf Chatel from Hazebrouck at 9 A.m.	
	29-3-16		Moved 12.30 P.m. to Merville	
	30-3-16		Pay to men 2·30 frs	

W W Buchanan Capt A.V.C.
O.C. 50th Mob Vet Sec

Army Form C. 2118.

WAR DIARY
or
INTELLIGENCE SUMMARY

(Erase heading not required.)

31st Mobile Vet. Section
39th Division Vol 2

Instructions regarding War Diaries and Intelligence Summaries are contained in F.S. Regs., Part II. and the Staff Manual respectively. Title Pages will be prepared in manuscript.

Place	Date	Hour	Summary of Events and Information	Remarks and references to Appendices
Trumilly	2/4/18	1pm	Evacuated 13 horses & 2 mules to N°13 Vet. Hospital Neufchatel	
do	8/4/18	3pm	Evacuated 22 horses to 13th Vet. Hospital Neuf Chatel	
do	13/4/18	10am	Evacuated 19 " to 13th Vet Hospital Neuf Chatel	
do	15/4/18	"	Evacuated 15 " to 13 Vet. Hospital Neuf Chatel	
do	16/4/18	5.30	Took the men of this Section	
do	19/4/18	9am	Left Trumilly en route for Goern. Arrived all day	
Goern	19/4/18	7pm	Arrived at Goern	
do	21/4/18	12.30	Evacuated 16 horses from Bethune Station to 13 Vet Hospt. Neuf Chatel	
do	27/4/18	7am	Evacuated 53 horses " " to 13 Vet Hospitals Neufchatel	
do	28/4/18	8.15pm	Alarm Bts. Many wounds of gas attack	
do	29/4/18		A & B mens out all day Etterbey. 148 horses left at Farm by various units	

Army Form C. 2118.

XXXIX Mobile Vet. Section
39th Division Vol 3

WAR DIARY
INTELLIGENCE SUMMARY
(Erase heading not required.)

Instructions regarding War Diaries and Intelligence Summaries are contained in F. S. Regs., Part II. and the Staff Manual respectively. Title Pages will be prepared in manuscript.

Place	Date	Hour	Summary of Events and Information	Remarks and references to Appendices
Front	1/3/16	2 pm	Capt Buchanan (Veterinary times) of E Squadron S.I.H. by Militia Dermal Saspersul mullaite	
"	2/3/16	9 am	"	
"	"	6 pm	Paid another visit to No. S.I.H. & found no re-acton	
"	4/3/16	11 am	Paid out this men of the Section	
"	6/3/16	11 am	Evacuated 22 horses to No. 13 Vet Hospl Neufchatel also medewed before dispatching & were re-vented	
"	7/3/16	"	1 man 1 mule settled to destroyed; cash received for same 210 Francs	
"	9/3/16	11 am	one stranded for man turnout on To R.O.O Railhead	
"	11/3/16	11 am	Capt Buchanan (Veterinary times) of 39 "Sig C" R.E. no re-actor	
"	12/3/16	11 am	Evacuated 31 horses & 2 mules to 13 Vet Hosp Neufchatel	
"	13/3/16	6 pm	Paid this men of the Section	
"	17/3/16	11 am	Evacuated 89 Horses to No 13 Vet Hosp Neufchatel	
"	21/3/16	10 am	Drew from Ordnance Stores ken Smiths Wands Horseshoes & various tools in the Division	
"	24/3/16	11 am	Evacuated 29 horses to No 13 Vet Hospital including one mare with foal at foot	
"	26/3/16	6.30	Paid this men of the Section	
"	7/3/16	—	71 3396 Pte Henry J. M. Promoted Corp &	
"	19/3/16	—	" 9312 Sgt Post promoted on leave of abouns to England for 9 days	
"	31/3/16	11 am	Evacuated 34 horses & one mule to No. 13 Veterinary Hospital	

A W Buchanan Capt AVC
OC 39 MVS

Army Form C. 2118

WAR DIARY
or
INTELLIGENCE SUMMARY
(Erase heading not required.)

50th Mobile Vet Section
June 1916
XXIX

Instructions regarding War Diaries and Intelligence Summaries are contained in F. S. Regs., Part II. and the Staff Manual respectively. Title Pages will be prepared in manuscript.

Place	Date	Hour	Summary of Events and Information	Remarks and references to Appendices
Given	3/6/16	2 pm	Inspected this Section on Monthly	
"	4/6/16	11 am	Evacuated 32 Sick Animals to No 13 Vet Hospital including 3 mules with Hurt at Vent	
"	"	4 pm	Section firing on the Rifle Range	
"	5/6/16	9 am	Section firing on the Rifle Range	
"	"	6 pm	Pte McHand Joined for duty from No 9 Veterinary Hospital	
"	"		Major Brown A.D.V.S. Proceeded on leave	
"	9/6/16	4:30 pm	Paid the Men of the Section	
"	10/6/16		Sergt Mundin (Saddlers Sergt) Proceeded to Envi Reserve Horse Depot Dieren	
"	11/6/16	10 am	Men of the Section firing on the Rifle Range	
"	12/6/16		Pte Boyd Joined for duty	
"	14/6/16	11 am	Evacuated 218 Sick Horses to No 13 Veterinary Hospital Neufchatel	
"	15/6/16		Pte Hunt & Pte Reynolds Proceeded on 9 days leave	
"	16/6/16		Pte Long & Pte Maners Transferred to No 15 Veterinary Hospital	
"	19/6/16		Pte Blain & Pte Manen Transferred to No 9 Veterinary Hospital	
"	21/6/16	11 am	Evacuated 20 horses & 3 mules to No 15 Veterinary Section Neufchatel	
"	23/6/16	2 pm	Capt Buchanan & the Sergt of Section Practice on the Range	
"	24/6/16	-	Pte Reynolds proceed on leave to England	
"	25/6/16	11 am	Evacuated 39 Horses & 2 Mules evacuated to No 13 Veterinary Hospital Neufchatel	

W.S. Buchanan Capt A.V.C.
O.C. 50 M.V.S.

Army Form C. 2118.

WAR DIARY
or
INTELLIGENCE SUMMARY

(Erase heading not required.)

50th Mobile Veterinary Section
July 1916
No. 39   Vol 1

Instructions regarding War Diaries and Intelligence Summaries are contained in F. S. Regs., Part II. and the Staff Manual respectively. Title Pages will be prepared in manuscript.

Place	Date	Hour	Summary of Events and Information	Remarks and references to Appendices
Goerri	3/7/16	noon	No 3304 Pte M Hunt tried by F.G.C.M. for absence without leave. Sentenced to 90 day F.P. No 1. 30 day remitted.	
"	5/7/16	noon	Evacuated 47 horses & 2 mules to No 13 Vet Hospital Neufchâtel	
"	8/7/16	6.30	About the mean of the Section	
"	9/7/16	9 am	Capt Green arrived at Bethune 10.20 am	
"	10/7/16		Capt Buchanan arrived returning from leave by aeroplane route	
"	12/7/16	noon	Evacuated 45 horses & 3 mules to Neufchâtel 13th Veterinary Hospital	
"	14/7/16		Sent 2 horses to be destroyed to Mme Graham Thomas Bethune receiving 330 frs	
"	15/7/16	10.30	Left Bethune arrived at Goerri 11.45	
"	19/7/16	7 am	Evacuated 33 horses & 2 mules to No 13 Veterinary Hospital Neufchâtel	
"	21/7/16	6.30	About the mean of the Section	
"	21/7/16	11.30 pm	Capt Buchanan called out to attend to sick horse belonging R.G.A.	
"	22/7/16	2 pm	Inspected the Section on jumping	
"	23/7/16	2 pm	Examined the Section and Mounted drill	
"	24/7/16	11 am	No 8169 Sgt Wright left to join 39th Division for duty	
"	26/7/16		Evacuated 30 horses & 6 mules to No 13 Veterinary Hospital Neufchâtel	
"	28/7/16	noon	Section at Mounted drill & jumping exercise	
"	29/7/16	2 pm	Section at Mounted drill & jumping exercise	
"	31/7/16		Run sheet of walk on turns trot to walk turns at the canter	

W.M. Buchanan Capt
O.C. 50 M.V.S.

Army Form C. 2118.

No. 39

WAR DIARY
or
INTELLIGENCE SUMMARY

50th Mobile Veterinary Section   August 1916

Vol 6

(Erase heading not required.)

Place	Date	Hour	Summary of Events and Information	Remarks and references to Appendices
Gezon	2-8-16	7.10am	Evacuated 3 5 horses & 2 mules to No 13 Veterinary Hospital Tinquetaint	
"	3-8-16	9.30pm	Capt Buchanan called out to two cases of Gas Horses	
"	4-8-16	6 am	Evacuated 4 horses & 1 mule from La Forge by Road - to No 23 Veterinary Hospital	
"	4-8-16	8pm	Paid the men of the Section	
"	5-8-16	2 pm	Section at Morrefield drill & gymkana	
"	9-8-16		Shoeing smith Scott well found absent at about 6.H. hours	
"	10-8-16	8 am	Evacuated 5 horses & 3 mules by Barge to No 23 Veterinary Hospital St-Omer.	
"	12-8-16	10.30am	Left Gezon by Route March for Sezincourt arrived Biercourt in time for the night, distant marching 12 horses	
"	13-8-16	9.30	Left Sezincourt arrived Le Quesnel 5 pm Traffic much, 12 hours	
Le Quesnel	15-8-16	11 am	Evacuated 20 horses & 2 mules to No 22 Veterinary Hospital Abbeville	
"	15-8-16	4 pm	Paid the men of the Section	
"	22-8-16	12 noon	Evacuated 37 horses & 4 mules to No 22 Vet Hospital Abbeville	
"	23-8-16	1.30am	Left Le Quesnelle arrived at Re-Bruxelle slept on the road	
Re Bruxelles	24-8-16	9 am	Left Re-Bruxelle arrived at Bruxelles 12 noon 116th Bde	
Bruxelles	25-8-16	9 am	Left Bruxelles arrived at St Leger 2pm Marched with the Brigade	
St Leger	26-8-16	9 am	Left St Leger arrived at Achieux at 10.45 am	
Achieux	26-8-16	2 pm	Evacuated 26 horses & 3 mules to No 1 Veterinary Hospital Forges-les-Eaux	
"	30-8-16		Established an advanced collecting station & the Horse & two men at Englebelmer	

W.H. Buchanan Capt A.V.C
O.C 50M V.S

Army Form C. 2118.

50th Mobile Veterinary Section
Sept 1916
Vol 7

WAR DIARY
or
INTELLIGENCE SUMMARY

(Erase heading not required.)

Instructions regarding War Diaries and Intelligence Summaries are contained in F. S. Regs., Part II. and the Staff Manual respectively. Title Pages will be prepared in manuscript.

Place	Date	Hour	Summary of Events and Information	Remarks and references to Appendices
Acheux	2.9.14	2 pm	Evacuated 16 sick horses & 9 mules to No 4 Veterinary Hospital Hurpe Les Carns	
"	4.9.14	4 pm	Evacuated first cattle disease from Englebelmer	
"	6.9.14	3 pm	Evacuated 30 horses & 9 mules to the 4 Veterinary Hospital	
"	"	6 pm	Took the Town of the Section	
"	9.9.14	2 pm	Evacuated 36 horses & 5 mules to Hurpe Les Carns No 4 Vet Hospital	
"	10.9.14		1 Serjt & 1 Private arrived for temporary duty	
"	12.9.14		Re arrival (above) arrived	
"	12.9.14	2.30	Evacuated 23 horses & 3 mules to No 4 Veterinary Hospital Hurpe-les-Carns	
"	13.9.14	6 pm	Took out the Town of the Section	
"	21.9.14	2 pm	Evacuated 23 horses & 3 mules to No 22 Veterinary Hospital Abbeville	
"	"		Owing to some Railway difficulty from the Somme was too far, arrangements were made	
"	24.9.14	2 pm	to Le Cange Station Conduit St Reges. The Cross Installation on Shapnoy Acgher Linet	
"	25.9.14	4 pm		
"	26.9.14	2 pm	Evacuated 23 horses & 2 mules to No 2 Veterinary Hospital D. Abbeville	
"	27.9.14	2 pm	Evacuated 23 horses & 2 mules to Abbeville 22 Veterinary Hospital	
"	29.9.14	2 pm	Evacuated 52 " " 3 " " Abbeville "	
"	29.9.16	6 pm	Took out the Town of the Section	
"	30.9.14	2 pm	Evacuated 35 horses 2 mules to No 22 Veterinary Hospital Abbeville	

W.H.Buchanan Cpt A.V.C
O.C 50 M.V.S.

Army Form C. 2118

WAR DIARY
or
INTELLIGENCE SUMMARY
(Erase heading not required.)

Instructions regarding War Diaries and Intelligence Summaries are contained in F. S. Regs., Part II. and the Staff Manual respectively. Title Pages will be prepared in manuscript.

Place	Date	Hour	Summary of Events and Information	Remarks and references to Appendices
Athens	17th		Visited M.V.S. 174th 116th 252nd R.F.A. general routine office work.	
	18th		" " " 179th Bde 184th	
	19th		" " " 59th F.D.C. 174th 116th R.F.A. general routine office	
	20th		" inspected 24 Lancers prior to embarkation, 2nd Surrey. Regt. general routine office work	
	21st		Visited M.V.S. 116th Inf Bde, 116th Bde, 174th Bde R.F.A. 252nd Bde R.F.A. Burra Sug. Visit. Received inspected remounts, 2 R.E. officers exam.	
	22nd		Conference with Veterinary officers prior to examination; examined 174th & 252nd Bde & 116th Bde R.F.A.	
	23rd		Visited M.V.S. inspected 30 horses, all new vetg officers, examined 15 off. selected for X.16. purposes.	
	24th		Visited 59th F.A.C. inspected horses for 3.16. purposes.	
	25th		50th M.V.S. general routine office work	
	26th		Visited 117th Inf Bde 116th Bde R.F.A. visited M.V.S. routine office	
	27th		Visited 179th 184th Bdes R.F.A. visited 59th F.A.C. M.V.S.	
	28th		Visited M.V.S. inspected 54 horses prior to examination, visited 174th M.V.S. Sug. Soug - Rec. train. inspected new steadings	
	29th		Visited M.V.S. inspected horses of 3q F.A.C. 116th Inf Bde, routine office work.	
	30th		Visited M.V.S. inspected horses, examined 174th & 252nd Indy Exp. held conference with very offs. general routine office work prior to examin. next	
	31st		Visited M.V.S. inspected 39 offrs horses.	
			F.A.C. 174th & 179th Bde R.F.A.	

Army Form C. 2118.

50" Mobile Veterinary Section Oct/Nov/16

WAR DIARY
or
INTELLIGENCE SUMMARY

(Erase heading not required.)

Instructions regarding War Diaries and Intelligence Summaries are contained in F. S. Regs., Part II. and the Staff Manual respectively. Title Pages will be prepared in manuscript.

Vol 8

Place	Date	Hour	Summary of Events and Information	Remarks and references to Appendices
Acheux	3-10-16	2 pm	Evacuated 14 Horses & 5 Mules to No 22 Veterinary Hospital Acheux	
"	3-10-16	2.30	Section moved to Hedauville arriving about 3.30 pm	
Hedauville	5-10-16	2 pm	Evacuated 14 Horses to No 22 Veterinary Hospital Acheux	
"	7-10-16	2 pm	Evacuated 33 Horses & 5 Mules to Acheux	
"	8-10-16	9 am	Section moved to Bouzincourt	
Bouzincourt	11-10-16	2 pm	Evacuated 55 horses & 9 mules to Acheux	
"	13-10-16	5 pm	Paid the men of this Section	
"	14-10-16	2 pm	Evacuated 20 horses & 6 mules to Acheux	
Hedauville	18-10-16	2 pm	No 1642 Pte Tenny A.V. granted special leave to England from 9/10/16 to 15/10/16	
Bouzincourt	"	"	Evacuated 45 H & 8 mules to Acheux	
"	"	"	Sergt King G. to men returned to No 1 Veterinary Hospital Heuze les Esven.	
"	21-10-16	"	Evacuated 15 horses & 1 mule to Acheux (evacuating 1 cart)	
"	22-10-16	"	Evacuated 8 horses to No 22 Vet Hospital Acheux	
"	25-10-16	2 pm	Evacuated 25 horses & 3 mules to No 22 Veterinary Hospital	
"	27-10-16		Commenced using horse rugs	
"	28-10-16	2 pm	Evacuated 20 horses & 1 mule to No 22 Veterinary Hospital	

W. Richardson, Capt.
A.C. 50 M. V. S.

Army Form C. 2118.

WAR DIARY
or
INTELLIGENCE SUMMARY
(Erase heading not required.)

Instructions regarding War Diaries and Intelligence Summaries are contained in F. S. Regs., Part II. and the Staff Manual respectively. Title Pages will be prepared in manuscript.

50th Mobile Veterinary Section
November 1916

Place	Date	Hour	Summary of Events and Information	Remarks and references to Appendices
Bruay	2.11.16	8.30am	Evacuated 23 horses & 3 mules to No 1 Veterinary Hospital Hesdin - by train. (sick mess attd.)	
"	5.11.16	"	Evacuated 6 & 3 horses + 3 mules to " " "	
"	7.11.16	"	" " " " "	
"	8.11.16	"	Sergt Gittings & 7 men moved from No 6 Vet Hospital for temporary duty	
"	"	"	Evacuated 64 horses to No 1 Veterinary Hospital Hesdin - by train	
"	9.11.16	9.30	Evacuated 33 horses & 3 mules to No 1 Veterinary Hospital	
"	10.11.16	10.am	Evacuated 72 horses to No 1 Veterinary Hospital	
"	11.11.16	"	Evacuated 32 horses to " 4 Veterinary Hospital	
"	14.11.16	11.am	Evacuated 36 horses & 1 mule to No 4 Veterinary Hospital	
"	15.11.16	"	Evacuated 15 horses to No 1 Veterinary Hospital	
"	16.11.16	8.am	Left en-route marched Bruival arriving about 3.30pm	
Bruival	18.11.16	11.am	Left at 11am marched to Candas entrained 1pm entrained at 4.30pm	
Esquelbecq	19.11.16		Arrived at Esquelbecq at 11am detrained & marched to Billet	
"	23.11.16		Major Barnes A.D.V.S. Evacuated on leave to England	
"	24.11.16		Capt Buchanan takes over duties of A.D.V.S.	
"	22.11.16		Indispector Pilot left the Section	
"	25.11.16		Evacuated 15 horses & 1 mule to No 23 Veterinary Hospital E. St Omer by train	

W H Buchanan Capt
O C 50th M V S

Army Form C. 2118.

30th Mobile Veterinary Section December 1916

Vol 10

WAR DIARY or INTELLIGENCE SUMMARY

(Erase heading not required.)

Instructions regarding War Diaries and Intelligence Summaries are contained in F. S. Regs., Part II. and the Staff Manual respectively. Title Pages will be prepared in manuscript.

Place	Date	Hour	Summary of Events and Information	Remarks and references to Appendices
Esquelbecq	2.12.16		Received from Roads Head & Remounts for distribution to Units	
"	3.12.16		Cnfte Henry admitted. No 134 Field Ambulance with fractured rib	
"	3.12.16		Three Surplus Sergl Drivers joined for temporary duty from RFA	
"	4.12.16	6.30	Evacuated 20 horses & 2 mules to No 23 Veterinary Hospital St Omer by Road	
"	5.12.16	"	Evacuated 16 horses to No 23 Veterinary Hospital St Omer by Road	
"	6.12.16	"	Evacuated 21 horses & 2 mules to No 23 Veterinary Hospital by rail	
"	7.12.16		No 52956 SSgt G Steven promoted A/SSgt vice Henry evacuated	
"	8.12.16		No 901 The Yc Day joined the section for duty	
"	"		1352 Pte E Gallagher transferred to No 8 Veterinary Hospital	
"	11.12.16		Evacuated 36 horses & me mule to No 23 Veterinary Hospital St Omer by Road	
"	11.12.16		Evacuated 4 Horses to St Omer by Motor Ambulance	
"	12.12.16		Evacuated 30 horses & St Omer by Road	
"	13.12.16		3 Surplus Sergl Drivers left for No 2 Veterinary Hospital Havre	
"	14.12.16			
"	15.12.16	9 am	Evacuated 9 horses to No 23 Veterinary Hospital St Omer by road	
"	15.12.16	11 am	SSgt Esquilting arrived Section 3 pm	
Watten	18.12.16 10.00		Evacuated 11 horses to No 23 Veterinary Hospital St Omer by Ambt (including 5 mange cases)	
"	"	"	No 10585 Sgt Broadbent SG AVC left for duty Chevail RFA 34 Division	
"	21.12.16	10 am	Evacuated 34 horses & 3 mules to No 23 Vet Hospital St Omer by road	
"	24.12.16		Cnfte Reside transferred to No 2 Vet Hospital Havre for duty with No 26 Veterinary Hospital	
"	25.12.16		Cnfte Buchanan G.50 MVS granted 10 days leave to England	
"	29.12.16		Lt F Marlow joined for duty from No 5 Veterinary Hospital	

E. Barraclough MRCVS
Lt OC 30 M.V.S

Army Form C. 2118.

WAR DIARY
or
INTELLIGENCE SUMMARY

(Erase heading not required.)

Veterinary Services

51st Mobile Veterinary Section January 1917

Instructions regarding War Diaries and Intelligence Summaries are contained in F. S. Regs., Part II. and the Staff Manual respectively. Title Pages will be prepared in manuscript.

Place	Date	Hour	Summary of Events and Information	Remarks and references to Appendices
Matau	2-1-17	10 am	Evacuated to 3 horses & 6 mules to No 23 Veterinary Hospital. Horses had contracted 11 horses sore.	
"	3-1-17		No 907 Pte X Day graded 10 days leave to England	
"	9-1-17		Evacuated 50 horses & 8 mules to No 23 Vet Hosp. 51 horses & 1 mule including 22 sore necks	
"	16-1-17		Evacuated 15 horses to No 23 Vet Hosp. 10 mange cases, 10 mange cases	
"	19-1-17		A/Capt Withers at 10 am arrived Salonique about 1 pm	
"	19-1-17		No 3379 S/S/ A/Cpl Haines G/ 1 hundred Supp	
"	19-1-17		" 4502 Pte A Green Awarded N.C.l Corps	
"	19-1-17		" 3349 S/S/ Sgt Haines G/ Transferred to No 51 Returning 9th Mule	
"	22-1-17		Evacuated 14 horses & 2 mules to No 23 Vet Hosp. 51 horses by rail (including 10 mange cases & new reinforcements)	
"	26-1-17		Paid the men of the Section	
"	28-1-17		Received instructions from ADVS XVII Corps evacuating and assuming under duties of the VIII Corps Horse disp. Officer under the Supervision of No. NPVS 51st Horse.	
"	30-1-17		On taking Mess Belat at Ghanghi the success Mule Horse Vet Sec. J. No. 51 Section was suffering from sandcracks in hooves. 25 Sick Animals, 14 of which were suffering from sandcracks. Troops amongst animals very hundred during the last two months. No Mules at present except one very good lot of mules & hears.	

W/B Colonel A/DVS XVIII Corps

Army Form C. 2118.

WAR DIARY
or
INTELLIGENCE SUMMARY

(Erase heading not required.)

50th M.V.S   Feb 1914

Vol 12

Instructions regarding War Diaries and Intelligence Summaries are contained in F. S. Regs., Part II. and the Staff Manual respectively. Title Pages will be prepared in manuscript.

Place	Date	Hour	Summary of Events and Information	Remarks and references to Appendices
Poperinghe	3.2.17		Horse Sergt A.V.C. reported from R.T.R reported for temporary duty	
"	5.2.17		Lt. Sullivan horse passed through VIII Corps home dep	
"	6.2.17		No 13853 Pte J. Ainsworth A.V.C. joined from No 23 Veterinary Hospital	
"	12.2.17		Evacuated 15 horse + 3 mules to No 23 Vet Hospital St Omer by rail including 5 mange cases	
"	13.2.17		Paid out the NCOs + men of the section	
"	19.2.17		Evacuated 5 2 horse + 1 mule to No 23 Vet Hospital St Omer by rail including 36 mange cases	little over.
"	20.2.17		Weather much milder, their out exercising horses returning to 3 days	
"			Sgt Spinoglio 10 am arrived at Ledringhem 3 pm. rained all day	
Ledringhem			8 cases of Stomatitis contagiose left by 55 Div mobile Vet Section	
"			Billets occupied here are very poor	
"	24.2.19		Evacuated 38 horses to No 23 Veterinary Hospital by road	
"	26.2.19		Evacuated 25 horses + 1 mule to No 23 Vet Hosp. St Omer	
"	28.2.17		Evacuated 2 horse to St Omer No 23 Vet Hosps by Road	
"			mange cases prevalent in this Division	
"			Clearing up all ground - also ready to hand over to Jalon mange WORMHOUDT	
"	27.2.19		Returned 8 cans of Stomatitis Contagiosa to 55 Div M.V.S	
"	20.2.17		Three A.V.C. Supplies Slips transferred to No 3 Vet Hospl Havre	

C.M.J. Dunbar Lieut A.V.C.
OC 50 M.V.S

Army Form C. 2118.

WAR DIARY
or
INTELLIGENCE SUMMARY

50th M.V.S.

March 1917

Vol 1

Instructions regarding War Diaries and Intelligence Summaries are contained in F.S. Regs., Part II. and the Staff Manual respectively. Title Pages will be prepared in manuscript.

(Erase heading not required.)

Place	Date	Hour	Summary of Events and Information	Remarks and references to Appendices
Fetchingham Poperinghe	1-3-17		Left Fetchingham 10-am arrived at Poperinghe 4-30 took over 20 animals from 33rd M.V.S. Billets very poor.	
"	2-3-17		Evacuated 2 Horses by Motor Ambulance to 23rd Vety. Hospital St Omer. Capt Buchanan took over the duties of A.D.V.S. whilst Major Sams sick.	
"	3-3-17		Evacuated 12 Animals to No 23 Vety. Hospital St Omer including 14 Cart.	
"	4-3-17		No 11303 Pte Hughes B. admitted to 13th Field Ambulance.	
"	5-3-17		" 2055 " Seal G. joined for duty from No 3 Vety Hospital.	
"	9-3-17		Capt Skelton A.V.C. takes over duties of 50th M.V.S.	
"	10-3-17		Evacuated 52 Horses 8 Mules to 23rd Vety. Hospital St Omer	
"	13-3-17		Evacuated 2 Mules to 23rd Vety. Hospital St Omer by Motor Ambulance	
"	14-3-17		Evacuated 2 Horses to 23rd Vety. Hospital St Omer by Motor Ambulance	
"	17-3-17		Evacuated 8 Horses 4 Mules to 23rd Vety. Hospital St Omer (Including Cofforage 1 Cart).	
"	21-3-17		Evacuated 1 Horse 1 Mule to 23rd Vety. Hospital St Omer by Motor Ambulance	
"	24-3-17		Evacuated 34 Horses 1 Mule to 23rd Vety. Hospital St Omer	
"	31-3-17		Evacuated 21 Horses 5 Mules to 28th Vety. Hospital St Omer	

Skelton Capt A.V.C.
O.C. 50th M.V.S.

WAR DIARY or INTELLIGENCE SUMMARY

Mot Vety Sec
April 1917

App 14

Place	Date	Hour	Summary of Events and Information	Remarks and references to Appendices
Poperinghe	3-4-17		Evacuated 3 Horses & 2 Mules by Train from Wippenhoek (Stavrinlaire)	
"	3-4-17		Capt Buchanan visited 186 Bde R.F.A. (Owing to V.O. 186 Bde R.F.A falling sick Capt Buchanan took over also)	
"	4-4-17		Capt Buchanan visited 186 Bde R.F.A.	
"	5-4-17		Major Barrus took over duties of A.D.V.S. 39th Division	
"	5-4-17		Capt Buchanan resumed duties as O.C. 50th M.V.S.	
"	7-4-17		Evacuated 13 Horses & Mules to 23rd Veterinary Hospital St Omer	
"	10-4-17		Moved from Poperinghe to Hazeele (billets bad and no covering for the Horses)	
Hazeele	12-4-17		Evacuated 1 Horse to 23rd Veterinary Hospital St Omer by Motor Transport	
"	12-4-17		Capt Buchanan visited 174 Bde R.F.A. (During the V.O.'s absence owing to illness Capt Buchanan took over also)	
"	12-4-17		Capt Buchanan took over charge of Units in the Rescue Area	
"	12-4-17 to 19-4-17		Capt Buchanan visited 174 Bde. R.F.A.	
"			Evacuated 10 Horses & 2 Mules to 23rd Veterinary Hospital St Omer	
"	18-4-17		Admitted 8 Animals from 298 Bde. Army F.A. (First animals were evacuated having just come from the Front)	
"	19-4-17		Great increase in animals, Capt Buchanan handing over charge to him (The Somme)	
"	20-4-17		Evacuated 12 Horses to 174 & 23rd Veterinary Hospital St Omer	
"	22-4-17		Evacuated 15 Horses to 23rd Veterinary Hospital St Omer	
"	23-4-17		Evacuated 2 Horses to 23rd Veterinary Hospital St Omer by Motor Ambulance	
"	23-4-17		Men had Gas drill, and marching drill	
"	24-4-17		Men had marching drill	
"	26-4-17		Evacuated 2 Horses to 23rd Veterinary Hospital St Omer by Motor Ambulance	
"	27-4-17		Men had marching drill.	
"	28-4-17		Evacuated 14 Horses and 3 Mules to 23rd Veterinary Hospital St Omer	
"	29-4-17		Pte Baylis granted Special Leave, owing to serious illness of Child	
"	29-4-17			R Buchanan Capt A.V.C. O.C. 50 M.V.S

Army Form C. 2118.

WAR DIARY
or
INTELLIGENCE SUMMARY 5 O Mot Vety Sec
(Erase heading not required.)

May 1917

Vol 15

Place	Date	Hour	Summary of Events and Information	Remarks and references to Appendices
Hengelo	1-5-17		Capt Buchanan visited No 1 Section 39th D.A.C.	
"	2-5-17		Evacuated 2 Horses to 23rd Veterinary Hospital St Omer, by Motor Ambulance	
"	2-5-17		Cpl. A. Lucas granted 30 days special leave.	
"	3-5-17		W.C.O and three men posted to VIII Corps Mobile Vet. detachment for duty.	
"	3-5-17		Section Paid.	
"	4-5-17		Capt Buchanan visited 225th Field Coy R.E.	
"	5-5-17		Capt Buchanan inspected horses for evacuation	
"	6-5-17		Evacuated 12 Horses and 2 mules to 23rd Veterinary Hospital St Omer	
"	10-5-17		Section had Rifle Inspection and Rifle Drill	
"	11-5-17		Section had Saddle Inspection	
"	12-5-17		Pte A. Baylis returned off leave.	
"	14-5-17		Capt Buchanan visited II Section 39th D.A.C. and III Section 53rd D.A.C.	
"	15-5-17		Capt Buchanan visited II Section 39th D.A.C.	
"	16-5-17		Evacuated 4 Horses to 23rd Veterinary Hospital St Omer	
"	16-5-17		Men had Section Drill	
"	16-5-17		Capt Buchanan visited II Section 53rd D.A.C., and III Section 53rd D.A.C, and 2nd Army Purchase Board.	
"	17-5-17		Section had gas Drill.	
"	18-5-17		Section had Saddle Inspection	
"	19-5-17		Section had Rifle Inspection	
"	20-5-17		Evacuated 10 Horses and 1 mule to 23rd Veterinary Hospital St Omer	
"	20-5-17		Capt Buchanan visited 116th Bde. Infantry, and II Section 39th D.A.C.	
"	20-5-17		Capt Buchanan visited 39th Divn Train, and II Section 39th D.A.C.	

WAR DIARY
or
INTELLIGENCE SUMMARY

(Erase heading not required.)

Army Form C. 2118.

MAY 1917.

Place	Date	Hour	Summary of Events and Information	Remarks and references to Appendices
HERZEELE	21-5-17		Evacuated 12 Horses and 1 Mule to O.C. 23rd Veterinary Hospital St Omer	
"	22-5-17		Capt Buchanan visited 116th Infantry Brigade, II Sect 39th O.M.G. III Coy Div Train & Horses of 2nd Army Purchase Board.	
"	23-5-17		Capt Buchanan visited 12th Sussex Regt, 14th Hants Regt, H.Q & 9/10 Batt. R.F.A. 2 Coy. Div Train.	
"	24-5-17		Men had instruction in the use of Horse Respirators, and also Anti-Gas Drill	
"	24-5-17		Establishment of Horses reduced by Nine, and Returned to Ordnance Saddlery for same.	
"	25-5-17		Section Paid	
"	25-5-17		Cleaned up the Camp, also Sectional Rifle Inspection.	
"	26-5-17		Capt Buchanan visited Troops in Wormhoudt	
"	28-5-17		Capt Buchanan visited Troops in Wormhoudt	
"	29-5-17		Capt Buchanan visited 116th Infantry Brigade and Section had Bath Parade.	
"	30-5-17		Capt Buchanan visited 118th Infantry Brigade, III Coy. 39th Div Train, and 2nd Army Purchase Board	
"	31-5-17		Evacuated 2 Horses to O.C. 23rd Veterinary Hospital St Omer	
"	31-5-17		Capt Buchanan visited 117th Infantry Brigade, IIII Coy. 39th Div Train, and 2nd Army Purchase Board	

WMBuchanan. Capt A.V.C.

O.C. 50th Coy. V.S.

Army Form C. 2118.

50th M.V.S.

Vol June 1917.

16

WAR DIARY
INTELLIGENCE SUMMARY
(Erase heading not required.)

Place	Date	Hour	Summary of Events and Information	Remarks and references to Appendices
Reninghelst	1/6/17		Section moved from Hazebrouck to A 27, C9-7 Sheet 27 near Reninghelst.	
"	2/6/17		Cpl. Jureo returned off leave.	
"	3/6/17		Pte. Cony AAJ and 11.30 Pte. Dodd J.H.H. sent from 8th Corps M.V.S. to report for duty with this Unit.	
"	4/6/17		Section had rifle inspection and drill, also saddle inspection.	
"	5/6/17		Capt. Buchanan proceeded to Reigersburg Chateau to get two mules (wounded).	
"	6/6/17		Mout proceeded to Vlamertinghe to fetch a horse. Section paid.	
"	7/6/17		Capt. Buchanan visited 39th Divisional Headquarters	
"	8/6/17		Capt. Buchanan visited 39th D.A.C.	
"	9/6/17		Evacuated 1 Horse, 1 Mule to 23rd Veterinary Hospital by Motor Ambulance. Cpl. Jarrad, Pte. Coney and Gould rejoined 8th Corps M.V.B. Capt. Buchanan visited 39th D.A.C.	
"	10/6/17		Evacuated 7 Horses & 4 Mules to 23rd Veterinary Hospital by Motor Ambulance. Evacuated 1 Horse, 1 Mule to 23rd Veterinary Hospital by Motor Ambulance.	
"	10/6/17		Sergt. Coldwell C. granted 10 days leave from 39th D.A.C. Capt. Buchanan visited 39th D.A.C.	
"	11/6/17		Capt. Buchanan visited 39th D.A.C.	
"	12/6/17		Capt. Buchanan visited Divl. Headquarters also 39th D.A.C.	
"	13/6/17		Capt. Buchanan visited 39th D.A.C. and found 30 Mules suffering from gas poison.	
"	14/6/17		Capt. Buchanan visited 39th D.A.C.	
"	15/6/17		Section had Rifle inspection and Saddle Inspection. Capt. Buchanan prepared animals for evacuation. Sgt. Coldwell C. promoted to Staff-Sergeant.	
"	16/6/17		Evacuated 8 Horses and 12 Mules to 28th Veterinary Hospital Et. Omer.	

2449 Wt. W14957/M90 750,000 1/16 J.B.C. & A. Forms/C.2118/12.

Army Form C. 2118.

50th MVS

WAR DIARY
INTELLIGENCE SUMMARY
(Erase heading not required.)

Place	Date	Hour	Summary of Events and Information	Remarks and references to Appendices
Ruitz	17-6-17		WO Inf/070532 Pte H. Blayden granted 10 days leave.	
"	19-6-17		Capt Buchanan proceeded to Reigersburg Château to get horse (wounded).	
"	19-6-17		Capt Buchanan proceeded to Steenvoorde to get horse (wounded)	
"	21-6-17		Men had Rifle Inspection and Saddle Inspection.	
"	22-6-17		Evacuated 1 Horse 1 Mule to 23rd Veterinary Hospital St Omer by Motor Ambulance	
"	22-6-17		Men had Gas Helmet Inspection and Drill.	
"	22-6-17		Capt Buchanan inspected animals for evacuation.	
"	22-6-17		Section Paid.	
"	23-6-17		Staff-Sergeant Caldwell G. returned off leave	
"	25-6-17		No. T.028 Sergt. T. Ruff reported for duty (in accordance with A.V.C. Rout Order 65 dated 15/6/17).	
"	26-6-17		Evacuated by rail 19 Horses and 5 Mules to No.13 Vety Hospital from 27/6/17 to 9/9/17.	
"	27-6-17		No.2755 Pte Floyd T.C. granted leave from 29th to 28th to Field Coy's R.E.	
"	28-6-17		Capt Buchanan visited 29th & 28th & Field Coy's R.E.	
"			Section paraded for Rations.	
"	29-6-17		Capt Buchanan visited 23rd Field Coy, R.E, and Reigersburg Château to examine wounded horses.	
"	29-6-17		Cpl Sloan proceeded in charge of Infant to Bergnette Farm to collect horse.	
"	29-6-17		WO Inf/070532 Pte H. Blayden returned from leave.	

MBuchanan
Capt. A.V.C.
O.C. 50th M.V.S.

Army Form C. 2118.

50th M.V.S. 39 Div.

WAR DIARY
or
INTELLIGENCE SUMMARY

(Erase heading not required.)

July 1917

Place	Date	Hour	Summary of Events and Information	Remarks and references to Appendices
Reubrock	2/7/17		Evacuated 27 Horses and 8 Mules to 28th Veterinary Hospital St Omer	
"	2/7/17		Evacuated 2 Horses to 23rd Vety: Hospital by Motor Ambulance (St Omer)	
"	2/7/17		Capt Buchanan visited 23rd Field Coy. R.E., also 227th Field Coy: R.E.	
"	3/7/17		Evacuated 1 Horse and 1 Mule to 23rd Vety: Hospital St Omer by Motor Ambulance.	
"	5/7/17		Capt Buchanan visited 234th Field Boy. R.E.	
"	6/7/17		Section Paid	
"	6/7/17		Capt Buchanan visited 39th Divisional Headquarters.	
"	10-7-17		Capt Buchanan took over duties as D.A.D.V.S, 39th Divn. while Major Keanes on leave.	
"	6-7-17		Evacuated 30 Horses and 6 Mules to 23rd Vety Hospital St Omer	
"	7-7-17		Float proceeded to 478 Field Coy. R.E. to get wounded animals.	
"	8-7-17		Float proceeded to 477 Field Coy. R.E. to get 1 wounded animal.	
"	9-7-17		Captain Buchanan visited I, II, III Sections 39th D.A.C.	
"	9-7-17		W.O 653 Pte MacDonald S. reported for duty.	
"	10-7-17		Evacuated 2 Horses to 23rd Veterinary Hospital by Motor Ambulance.	
"	13-7-17		Capt Buchanan visited 15th Corps Horse Camp.	
"	13-7-17		Evacuated 2 Horses to 23rd Veterinary Hospital by Motor Ambulance	
"	14-7-17		Capt Buchanan visited and attended to wounded animals belonging to 39th Signals R.E.	
"	12-7-17		Capt Buchanan visited the Area Commandant.	
"	11-7-17		Capt Buchanan admitted 6 animals belonging to 46th Heavy Artillery Group R.G.A. for 24 hr's supervision.	
"	11-7-17		Evacuated 1 Horse and 1 Mule to 23rd Veterinary Hospital St Omer by Motor Ambulance.	
"	13-7-17		Capt Buchanan visited 17th Coy's Horse dép	
"	14-7-17		W.O 2788 Pte T.G. Lloyd returned off Leave (Granted 5 days extension)	

WAR DIARY
or
INTELLIGENCE SUMMARY

Army Form C. 2118.

July 1917 50th M.V.S. 39th

Place	Date	Hour	Summary of Events and Information	Remarks and references to Appendices
Poelcock	15/7/17		Capt Buchanan visited 18th Corps Horse Dip.	
"	15/7/17		Capt Buchanan visited I, II & III Sections 39th D.A.C.	
"	15/7/17		Motor Ambulance and Section Float proceeded to PROVEN with sick animals.	
"	16/7/17		Float proceeded to PROVEN with sick animals.	
"	17/7/17		Evacuated 26 Horses and 1 Mules to No 13 Veterinary Hospital Neufchatel	
"	17/7/17		Capt Buchanan visited 15th Corps Horse Dip.	
"	18/7/17		Capt Buchanan visited Labour Coy. at PROVEN. and 18th Corps Horse Dip	
"	19/7/17		Capt Buchanan visited Field Collns 39th Divisional Headquarters	
"	19/7/17		Major Barn returned off leave, Capt Buchanan resumed duties as O.C. 50th V.S. and W.O. 39 & 9. a. C.	
"	20/7/17		Evacuated 32 Horses and 7 mules to No 23 th Veterinary Hospital at Grew	
"	21/7/17		Capt Buchanan proceeded to Goal Bank YPRES.	
"	22/7/17		Capt Buchanan visited I, II & III Section 39th D.A.C.	
"	24/7/17		Capt Buchanan killed by shell on the night of 24/7/17, also WO 9312 Sergt Partrey wounded.	
"	24/7/17		Capt Shelton takes over duties as O.C. 50th M.V.S.	
"	25/7/17		Evacuated 1 Horses and 13 Mules to 18th Corps. M.V.D.	
"	25/7/17		Evacuated 5 Horses and Capt Shelton visited 39th Divisional Train	
"	26/7/17		Evacuated 6 Horses and 3 Mules to 18th Corps. M.V.D. and Capt Shelton visited 132, 133, 134 Field Amb.	
"	27/7/17		Capt Shelton visited 39th Divisional Headquarters and Capt Shelton visited 39th Sig. Train.	
"	27/7/17		Evacuated 3 Horses to 18th Corps. M.V.D.	
"	29/7/17		Capt Shelton visited 39th Divg. Train; and 132, 133, 134 Field Ambulance.	
"	30/7/17		Evacuated 4 Horses and 1 Mule to XVIII Corps. M.V.D.	

Army Form C. 2118.

WAR DIARY
or
INTELLIGENCE SUMMARY
(Erase heading not required.)

July 1917   50th M.V.S.   39 Div

Place	Date	Hour	Summary of Events and Information	Remarks and references to Appendices
Pawlerk	29/7/17		Evacuated 18 Horses and 3 Mules to XVIII Corps M.V.D.	
"	30/7/17		Capt Shelton visited 39th Divisional Train.	
"	30/7/17		Capt Shelton visited 133rd & 134th Field Ambulance, and No 317 Sergt Wright T. joined for duty.	
"	31/7/17		Evacuated 3 Horses to XVIII Corps M.V.D.	
"	31/7/17		Capt Shelton visited 39th Divisional Train, and 135 Field Ambulance	

Shelton Capt A.V.C.

O.C. 50th M.V.S.

D.A.D.V.S.,
39TH DIVISION.
No. YM/176
Date 31/8/17

Army Form C. 2118.
D.A.D.V.S.
89TH DIVISION

No. ....

50th M.V. Section

WAR DIARY
or
INTELLIGENCE SUMMARY
(Erase heading not required.)

Instructions regarding War Diaries and Intelligence Summaries are contained in F. S. Regs., Part II. and the Staff Manual respectively. Title Pages will be prepared in manuscript.

Place	Date	Hour	Summary of Events and Information	Remarks and references to Appendices
Reninghelst	1/5/17		Capt Shelton visited 132, 132B, 134 Field Ambulance.	
"	2/5/17		Capt Shelton visited 39th Divisional Train.	
"	2/6/17		Capt Shelton visited Field Cashier 39th Div. Headquarters.	
"	2/6/17		Evacuated 4 Horses and 1 Mule to XVIII Corps M.V.D.	
"	2/7/17		Capt Shelton visited 132, 133, 134 K Field Ambulance	
"	3/7/17		Evacuated 7 Horses and 2 Mules to XVIII Corps M.V.D.	
"	4/5/17		Capt Shelton visited 132, 133, 134 Field Ambulance, and 39th Divisional Train.	
"	4/5/17		Evacuated 4 Horses to XVIII Corps M.V.D.	
"	5/5/17		Evacuated 7 Horses and 3 Mules to XVIII Corps M.V.D.	
"	5/8/17		Capt Shelton visited 132, 133, 134 Field Ambulance	
"	6/8/17		Evacuated 2 Horses and 2 Mules to XVIII Corps M.V.D.	
"	6/8/17		Capt Shelton visited 132, 133, 134 Field Ambulance.	
"	6/8/17		No 3703 Pte Hunt M. granted leave (19 days)	
"	7/8/17		Evacuated 1 Horse and 2 Mules to XVIII Corps M.V.D.	
"	7/8/17		Evacuated 1 Horse to XVIII Corps M.V.D.	
Boeschepe	8/8/17		Moved to R.21.a.5.3 sheet 27 u.2 Rotten	
"	9/8/17		Capt Shelton visited 39th Divisional Headquarters	
"	10/8/17		Capt Shelton visited Field Cashier Bailleul	
"	10/8/17		Section Paid.	
"	12/8/17		Capt Shelton visited Field Ambulance and 13th Afmeries	
"	13/8/17		Capt Shelton visited 39th Divisional Headquarters	
"	14/8/17		Section moved to N-7.a.5.5 sheet 28. LA CLYTTE.	

2449 Wt. W14957/Mg0 750,000 1/16 J.B.C. & A. Forms/C.2118/12.

WAR DIARY or INTELLIGENCE SUMMARY

Army Form C. 2118.
50th M.V. Section
89th DIVISION

Place	Date	Hour	Summary of Events and Information	Remarks and references to Appendices
La Clytte	15/8/17		Capt Shelton examined about 40 sick animals taken over from 52nd M.V.S.	
"	16/8/17		Capt Shelton visited 117th Infantry wagon lines	
"	17/8/17		Evacuated 25 Horses and 11 Mules to No 23 Vety. Veterinary Hospital	
"	17/8/17		Notification received that S.S. Kenry R.f. promoted to P/A/S.S. Corporal with effect from 11/8/17	
"	17/8/17		Captain Shelton visited 1st Lincolns, Kings(L'pool) Company	
"	19/8/17		Captain Shelton visited 13th Gloucesters & 133rd Field Ambulance	
"	20/8/17		Captain Shelton visited 19 Horses and 26 Mules to No 23rd Veterinary Hospital	
"	20/8/17		Capt Shelton visited 132,133 Field Ambulance	
"	21/8/17		Evacuated (9 - Total) 17 Horses and 7 Mules to WO 10 Vety. Hospital	
"	22/8/17		Capt Shelton visited 133 Field Ambulance	
"	23/7/17		Capt Shelton visited 119 Bde. R.F.A.	
"	24/8/17		Section Paid. Capt Shelton visited 175 Tunnelling Coy.	
"	25/8/17		WO 18820 S.S. Parkinson A. reported for duty	
"	26/8/17		1 W.C.O and 3 Men detailed to 1/X Gp's M.V.D. for duty	
"	26/7/17		Captain Shelton Inf and horses for evacuation	
"	26/7/17		Captain Shelton visited 132,133 Field Ambulances	
"	27/7/17		Evacuated 44 Horses and 4 Mules to WO 23 Veterinary Hospital	
"	29/7/17		WO 10201 S/S /Cpl Kenry G.F. despatched to WO 14 Veterinary Hospital for duty	
"	30/8/17		Capt Shelton visited 11th Welch Fus. A.T.G.	
"	30/7/17		Evacuated 9 Horses and 3 Mules to WO 10 Vety. Hospital	

Shelton
Capt. Q.V.G.
O.C. 50th M.V.S.

Capt Q.V.G.
O.C. 50th M.V.S.

WAR DIARY
or
INTELLIGENCE SUMMARY

Army Form C. 2118.

50 Mob Vety Sec Vol 19

Place	Date	Hour	Summary of Events and Information	Remarks and references to Appendices
Po, Cype	1/9/17		1 Mule sent to DESOHILDRE FRERES BAILLEUL for Slaughter	
"	2/9/17		Evacuated 32 Horses and 3 Mules to HAEGEDOORNE	
"	3/9/17		Evacuated 56 Horses and 4 Mules to 23rd Veterinary Hospital St-Omer	
"	4/9/17		Evacuated 1 Horse to Xth Corps M.V.D. Capt Shellen visited 39 D.H.Q. visited 39 D.H.Q. 112 Infantry Brigade	
"	5/9/17		Capt Shellen visited 39 D.H.Q. also 112 Infantry Brigade	
"	5/9/17		Evacuated 3 Horses to Xth Corps M.V.D.	
"	5/9/17		Evacuated 18 Animals G+S, 1 y to 23rd Veterinary Hospital St-Omer	
"	6/9/17		Evacuated 4 Horses to Xth Corps M.V.D. Capt Shellen visited 36th M.V.S.	
"	7/9/17		Capt Shellen visited Field Canbul RENINGHELST, also 39th D.H.Q. and 133 Field Ambulance	
"	7/9/17		Evacuated 4 Horses to Xth Corps M.V.D.	
"	8/9/17		2 Mules (found straying) sent to Field Remount Section.	
"	8/9/17		Evacuated 15 Horses and 4 Mules to 1st Anzac Vety. C.C.S.	
"	8/9/17		Capt Shellen prepared Knees for evacuation.	
"	8/9/17		WO 18722 Pte Andrews, G.E. admitted to 133 Field Ambulance.	
"	9/9/17		Cpl Lucas, A. detailed to proceed to Xth Corps M.V.D. to relieve Sgt Ralf, T.J.	
"	9/9/17		1 Mule sent to DESGHILDRE FRERES for Slaughter (BAILLEUL)	
"	9/9/17		Capt Shellen visited 39 D.H.Q. also Special Section.	
"	9/9/17		Cpl Lucas, A. returned from Xth Corps M.V.D.	
"	10/9/17		Evacuated 25 Horses & 4 Mules to 23 Veterinary Hospital St-Omer, & Capt Shellen visited 6th M.V.S.	
"	10/9/17		1 W.G.O. & 2 men detailed to 23 Vet. Hospital St-Omer for course of clipping	
"	11/9/17		Evacuated 1 Horse to Xth Corps M.V.D.	
"	11/9/17		WO 12722 Pte Andrews, G.E. returned from 133 Field Ambulance	

WAR DIARY
or
INTELLIGENCE SUMMARY

Army Form C. 2118.

Place	Date	Hour	Summary of Events and Information	Remarks and references to Appendices
La Clytte	1/9/17		1 Mule sent to BESCHILDRE FRERES RAINEUR for slaughter	
"	2/9/17		Evacuated 32 Horses and 3 Mules to HAEGEDOORNE	
"	3/9/17		Evacuated 56 Horses and Mules to 23rd Vety. Hospital St Omer.	
"	4/9/17		Evacuated 1 Horse to F. Coys. M.V.D. Capt Shelton visited 39th D.H.&	
"	5/9/17		Capt Shelton visited 39th D.H.Q. also 112th Infantry Brigade	
"	5/9/17		Evacuated 3 Horses to F. Coys M.V.D.	
"	5/9/17		Evacuated 15 Animals "GASTD to 23rd Veterinary Hospital St Omer	
"	6/9/17		Evacuated 4 Horses to F. Coys M.V.D. Capt Shelton visited 38 & 39th M.V.S.	
"	7/9/17		Capt Shelton visited Mobile Section RENINGHELST, also 39th D.H.Q. and 133, Field Ambulance	
"	7/9/17		Evacuated 4 Horses to F. Coys. M.V.D.	
"	7/9/17.		2 Mules (found straying) sent to Field Remount Section.	
"	8/9/17		Evacuated 15 Horses and Mules to 12th Auxre Vety. C.C.S.	
"	8/9/17		Capt Shelton Inspected Lorry for evacuation.	
"	8/9/17		No.13722 Pte Hopman, G.E. admitted to 133, Field Ambulance	
"	9/9/17		Cpl Lucas. A. detailed to proceed to F. Coys M V D to relieve Sgt. Ralf. T. J.	
"	9/9/17		1 Mule sent to DESCHILDRE FRERES for slaughter. (BAILLEUL)	
"	9/9/17		Capt Shelton visited 39th D.H.Q. also paid Section.	
"	9/9/17		Cpl Lucas A. returned from F. Coys. M.V.D.	
"	10/9/17		Evacuated 25 Horses & Mules to 23, Veterinary Hospital St Omer, Capt Shelton visited 38 & 39 M.V.S.	
"	10/9/17		1 W.O.O and 2 men dispatched to 23 Vet. Hospital St Omer, for course of clipping	
"	11/9/17		Evacuated 1 Horse to F. Coys M.V.D. from 133, Field Ambulance	

WAR DIARY or INTELLIGENCE SUMMARY

Army Form C. 2118.

Instructions regarding War Diaries and Intelligence Summaries are contained in F. S. Regs., Part II. and the Staff Manual respectively. Title Pages will be prepared in manuscript.

(Erase heading not required.)

Place	Date	Hour	Summary of Events and Information	Remarks and references to Appendices
La Bassée	28/9/17		Handed over 12 animals to 28th Mobile Vet. Section	
St Jans Cappel	29/9/17		Section moved to St Jans Cappel	
"	29/9/17		1 Man returned from X. Corps' M.V.D.	
"	29/9/17		Capt Skelton visited 39th D.H.Q.	
"	30/9/17		Capt Skelton visited 39th D.H.Q.	

Capt A.V.C.
O.C. 50th M.V.S.

WAR DIARY or INTELLIGENCE SUMMARY

Army Form C. 2118.

Mob Vety Sec 50th M.V.S.

October 1917

Vol 20

Place	Date	Hour	Summary of Events and Information	Remarks and references to Appendices
St Jans Cappel	1/10/17		Evacuated 1 Horse to 4th Corps M.V.D.	
St Jans Cappel	2/10/17		Capt Skelton granted leave.	
"	2/10/17		Major Barnes D.A.D.V.S. 39th Divn acting as O.C. 50th M.V.S.	
"	5/10/17		WO 9786 Pte Wilson W.G. granted 10 days leave.	
"	5/10/17		1 Horse sent to Boulogne Horse of Peached for slaughter.	
"	6/10/17		WO 10700 Pte Woodland R.H. granted 10 days leave.	
"	6/10/17		Major Barnes left and animals for evacuation.	
"	7/10/17		WO 8256 Cpl Sloman A.W. returned from leave.	
"	7/10/17		Evacuated 27 Horses + 10 Mules to 23rd Vet Hospital St Omer (included were 2 Horses + 14 Mule CAST and 6 Horses + 5 Mules from IX Corps M.V.S.)	
"	7/10/17		Section paraded for baths.	
"	11/10/17		WO 10941 Pte Wallis A.G. granted leave from 12-10-17 to 22-10-17.	
"	14/10/17		Evacuated 14 Horses and 3 Mules to 23rd Vet Hospital.	
"	14/10/17		Sent 1 CAST. Horse to Field Remount Station.	
"	14/10/17		WO 5615 Pte Morehart S. granted leave from 15-10-17 to 25-10-17.	
"	16/10/17		WO 9786 Pte Wilson W.G. returned from leave.	
"	16/10/17		Handed over 3 animals to 28th M.V.S.	
DEVISES CAMP	16/10/17		Section moved to Devises Camp.	
"	17/10/17		WO 10700 Pte Woodland R.H. returned from leave. WO S.E.8256 Cpl Sloman A.W. admitted to Hospital 3/10/17.	
"	18/10/17		WO 7583 Pte Bromley H. granted leave from 20/17-17 to 7th Corps G.G.S.	
"	19/10/17		Evacuated 1 Horse & 1 Mule to	

WAR DIARY or INTELLIGENCE SUMMARY

Army Form C. 2118.

50 M.V.S.

Place	Date	Hour	Summary of Events and Information	Remarks and references to Appendices
Divisional Camp	21/10/17		Evacuated Horses & 2 Mules to No 23 Veterinary Hospital. Str. Owl	
"	22/10/17		Capt. Sheller R.F. returned from leave and resumed duties as O.C.	
"	23/10/17		No 12782 Pte. Irons. R.E. Dental Leave from 23/10/17 to 2/11/17.	
"	24/10/17		Evacuated 2 Horses 1 Mule to F.O. Corps Vety. C.C.S.	
"			No 9508 Pte. Hawkins D.R. granted leave from 26/10/17 to 10/11/17.	
"	27/10/17		Cpl. Jones. A. sent to the Artillery Ride to superintend shifting of Horses	
"	29/10/17		Capt. Storm evacuated	
"	20/10/17		70552 Dr. Tony A.V.S. transferred to (1) Veterinary men Storm / Supervision marked 125 men & 1 mule	
"	20/10/17		Sgt. Duff and Four men D.O. to Tanks Corps. 7th Detachment. Sgt. Duff returned	
"	26/10/17		Re Merchant returned from Leave	
"	27/10/17		Capt. Sheller visited D.M.L. Wing to enable to field Ambul Purveyors	
"	28/10/17		Prepared Horses for Evacuation	
"	28/10/17		I visited Tanks Corps mobile Workshops regarding repairs to front	
"			Procured 4 such Horses. Eight mules and three Gun Horses. 25 Vet. Hosp. Str. Owl.	
"			Monthly evaluation detachment out there regarding repairs to flanks	
"	29/10/17		No 11634 Pte Barrett A.V. granted leave from 30/10/17 to 9/11/17.	
"			" 31756 Grs. Frith. att 50th M.V.S. Granted leave from 31/10/17 to 10/11/17.	
"	30/10/17		" 17M059872 Ds. Mansfield att 50th M.V.S. Granted leave from 31/10/17 to 10/11/17.	
"	31/10/17			

J Gillson
Capt AVC
O.C. 50 M.V.S.

WAR DIARY
INTELLIGENCE SUMMARY

Army Form C. 2118.
D.A.D.V.S. 50th Div.

50th M.V.S.

VA 21

Place	Date	Hour	Summary of Events and Information	Remarks and references to Appendices
Devises Camp	Nov 1		Evacuated 10 Horses & 2 Mules to I Corps C.C.S. Pte Bromley 71077683 Returned from Leave	
"	2		Evacuated 2 Horses & one Mule to I Corps C.C.S.	
"	3		Evacuated 3 Horses & 4 Mules to N°13 Vety Hospital Neufchâtel	
"	4		Evacuated 6 Horses 9 4 Mules to IX Corps C.C.S. Evacuated 39 Horses & 9 Mules to 23 Vet Hospt St Omer	
"	5		Refused Horses & Mules for Evacuation	
"	6		Evacuated 7 Horses & 3 Mules to I Corps C.C.S. Visited Field Cashers	
"	7		Visited Stripping Station of Division & B.H.Q. Pte Meachins N°9503 Returned from Leave	
"	8		Evacuated 21 Horses & 3 Mules 9 7 Mules to IX Corps C.C.S. Ref Mayt. Visited D.H.Q. and Stripping Statn	
"	9		Visited D.H.Q. 2nd Stripping Statn	
"	10		Evacuated 4 Horses to 1st August I.C.C.S. Refused Horses for Evacuation	
"	11		Evacuated 12 Horses to N°23 Vet Hospt St Omer. Pte Barrett N°11854 Returned from leave	
"	12		Sgt Ref T.Y. N°7028 Granted leave from 13-11-17 to 27-11-17 Pte Brown 3/E/11722 Returned from Leave	
"	13		Refused Horses for Evacuation	
"	14		Evacuated 26 Horses 9 7 Mules to IX Corps M.V.D	
"	15		4 Men sent for Duty at IX Corps M.V.D Evacuated 7 Horses to IX Corps M.V.D	
"	16		Dr Mansfield M.R.C.V.S. 2548972 Returned from Leave. Gnr A Fuche 21731786 Returned from leave	

WAR DIARY
INTELLIGENCE SUMMARY.
(Erase heading not required.)

Army Form C.2118.

50th MYS

Place	Date	Hour	Summary of Events and Information	Remarks and references to Appendices
	Nov.			
Devises Camp	16		Evacuated 2 Horses and 1 Mule to IX Corps M.V.D. Prepared Horses for Evacuation	
"	17		Evacuated 23 Horses & 8 Mules to N°23 Vet. Hospital St. Omer	
"	"		Evacuated 2 Horses to IX Corps M.V.D	
"	18		Evacuated 2 Horses to IX Corps M.V.D	
"	19		Evacuated 4 Horses and 1 Mule to IX Corps M.V.D. Staff Sgt. Smith reported for duty	
"	"		Pte DODD D.H.T.D. 11630 returned from leave	
"	21		Evacuated 4 Horses to IX Corps M.V.D. Visited Corps H.Q. Pte Reynolds Released from Leave	
"	22		Visited Divisional H.Q. Train H.Q. 913 & Field Ambulances	
"	23		Prepared animals for Evacuation. Evacuated 1 Mule to IX Corps M.V.D	
"	24		Evacuated 35 Horses, 9 Mules to N°23 Vet Hosp't. St O. was Visited D.H.Q.	
"	"		Pte Jeffery N° 223772 granted Leave from 24-11-17 to 8-12-17. Visited D.H.Q	
"	"		Evacuated 3 Horses to IX Corps M.V.D Visited D.H.Q	
"	26		Evacuated Devises Camp. Visited D.H.Q	
"	"		Arrived in camp at Morbecque Visited D.H.Q	
"	27		Visited D.H.Q. VIII Corps Mobile Vet Sect	
"	28		Sgt Ruff 2077.028 Returned from leave Visited D.H.Q	

WAR DIARY
or
INTELLIGENCE SUMMARY

50ᵗʰ M.V.S.

Army Form C.2118.

Place	Date	Hour	Summary of Events and Information	Remarks and references to Appendices
Wulton	Nov 29		Prepared Horses for Evacuation. Received D.11.Q.	
"	30		Evacuated 24 Horses and 4 Mules to 7ᵗʰ 23 Vet Hospt St Omer.	
"	30		Visited D.H.Q.	

O/C 50ᵗʰ Mob Vety Sect.

WAR DIARY
or
INTELLIGENCE SUMMARY.

Army Form C. 2118.

50th M.V.S.
December 1917

Vol 2

Place	Date	Hour	Summary of Events and Information	Remarks and references to Appendices
Watou	1/12/17		Visited 39th D.H.Q.	
"	2/12/17		No 317 Sgt Wright A.V.C. proceeded on leave. No 4025 Pte Martin returned off leave.	
"	3/12/17		Capt Shelton visited 39th D.H.Q.	
"	4/12/17		Visited 39th D.H.Q.	
"	5/12/17		No 653 Pte Macdonald A.V.C. proceeded on leave. Visited 39th D.H.Q.	
"	6/12/17		Visited Field Central D.H.Q. and obtained animals for evacuation	
"	7/12/17		Evacuated 21 Horses and 6 Mules to 23 Veterinary Hospital St Omer	
"	9/12/17		Section Moved to Nieurlet – leg – Belgium	
Nieurlet Belgium	11/12/17		27305 Pte Walker proceeded on leave. No 9596 Pte Owen N.Y. joined from No 2 Veterinary Hospital	
"	12/12/17		223712 Pte EA Jeffery returned off leave.	
"	13/12/17		Evacuated 6 Horses & 1 Mule to 23 Vet Hospital St Omer. 4 men returned to 236 Employment Coy.	
"	17/12/17		No 317156 Pnr Simpson R.F.A. (att. 50th M.V.S.) proceeded on leave. Visited Field Central.	
"	19/12/17		No 317 Sgt Wright A.V.C. returned off leave.	
"	20/12/17		No 762 Cpl Coney proceeded on leave. Evacuated 3 Horses & 1 Mule to 23 Vet Hospital St Omer.	
"	21/12/17		Section Paid.	

Army Form C. 2118.

WAR DIARY
or
INTELLIGENCE SUMMARY.
(Erase heading not required.)

December 1917

Instructions regarding War Diaries and Intelligence
Summaries are contained in F. S. Regs., Part II.
and the Staff Manual respectively. Title pages
will be prepared in manuscript.

Place	Date	Hour	Summary of Events and Information	Remarks and references to Appendices
Millebeque	23/12/17		No 653 Pte MacDonald A.V.C returned off leave	
"	24/12/17		10 men arrived for duty from No 2 Veterinary Hospital	
"	26/12/17		10 men dispatched to No 2 Veterinary Hospital. Evacuated 5 Horses 1 Mule to 23 Vet. Hospital St Omer	
"	27/12/17		No 27305 Pte Walker returned off leave	
"	28/12/17		No 14709 Pte Gibson A.V.C proceeded on leave	
"	29/12/17		No 2706 Pte Smith A.V.C. Evacuated 1 Horse 1 Mule to 23 Vet Hospital St Omer.	
"	30/12/17		35407 Rfn Lovell 17th K.R.R. (Att to 50th M.V.S) proceeded on leave	
"	31/12/17		Moved from Millebeque-lez-Aliquin to St Momelin	
St Momelin	31/12/17		Moved to St Froilan-Burgen	

Capt AVC
O i/c 50th M.V.S.

WAR DIARY or INTELLIGENCE SUMMARY

Army Form C. 2118.

50 Mob Vety Sec
January 1918

Vol 23

Place	Date	Hour	Summary of Events and Information	Remarks and references to Appendices
A28 C2.6	1/1/18		Moved from St Maulin to St Jnots Birgen	
	2/1/18		Moved from St Jnots Birgen to A28 C2-6. Sheet 28.	
	3 "		2 men inoculated to II Corps M.V.S. Gnd Surgeon H. returned off leave.	
	4 "		Ghost sent to Canal bank for animal. Visited 7th & 9th Batt. Can. Railway Troops.	
	5 "		No 212477 Pte Whitcombe T. proceeded on leave.	
	6 "		No 762 Cpl Conry A.I.F. returned off leave. Visited 7th & 9th Batt. Can. Railway Troops and 1334 134 Field Ambulance. Profahud horses for evacuation Pte Brown. G.S. (236 Emp. Coy) att 50th M.V.S. sent to II Corps School of Sanitation for course.	
	7 "		Evacuated 36 Horses and 7 Mules to Railhead PESELHOEK. About sent to 7/174 Rele K.F.A. for animal. Visited Field Cookers. Visited 39th D.N.D., 134 Field Ambulance & 749 Batt. Can. Railway Troops. Section Parade	
	9 "		No 762 Cpl Conry A.I.F. sent to II Corps M.V.S.	
	10 "		Visited 39th D.N.D., 134 Field Ambulance and 7th & 9th Batt. Can. Railway Troops.	
	11 "		No 1642 Cpl Lucas A. returned off leave.	
	12 "		Evacuated 13 H.D. (CAST) Horses to 2nd Army Field Remount Section. Visited 3rd Traffic Control Squadron and 7th & 9th Batt. Can. Railway Troops.	
	13 "		No 18820. S. Smith Rackman A. proceeded on leave. No 14709 Pte Gibson T. ret. off leave. Profahud horses for evacuation. Ret through G.A. returned off Sanitation course at II Corps School.	
	14 "		Evacuated 20 Horses, 7 Mules (9-17 Mules) to a Veterinary Hospital Q41 A1.S.	

Army Form C. 2118.

WAR DIARY
or
INTELLIGENCE SUMMARY

January 1918.

(Erase heading not required.)

Instructions regarding War Diaries and Intelligence Summaries are contained in F.S. Regs., Part II. and the Staff Manual respectively. Title Pages will be prepared in manuscript.

Place	Date	Hour	Summary of Events and Information	Remarks and references to Appendices
A 26 b2-6 Sht 28	15th		No 2706 Pte Smith G.W. returned off leave. No 35407 Rfm Jones R.S. returned off leave.	
	16th		Visited 7 & 9th Batt. Gen. Rail. Troops and 3rd Traffic Control Squadron.	
	17th		Visited 133 & 134 Field Ambulance.	
	18th		Visited 7 & 9th Batt. Gen. Rail. Troops and 3rd Traffic Control Squadron.	
	20th		Prepared Horses for evacuation. Visited 7 & 9th Batt. Gen. Railway Troops and 3rd Traffic Control Squadron.	
	21st		Evacuated 44 Horses and Totules to Railhead Roulleck. No 27277 Rfm Whitecake T.A. returned off leave.	1 N.B.O. & others returned from
	22nd		Moved to PROVEN.	
PROVEN	23rd		Sent two animals to "11" Coys. M.V.D.	
	24th		Sent 1 animal to "11" Coys M.V.D.	
"	26th		Moved to MERCOURT. No 2722 Pte Brown G.E. proceeded on leave.	
MERCOURT	29th		Rifle Inspection. Gas drill and lecture by 39th Divs. Gas N.C.O.	
	29th		No 25031 Pte Myratt N.B. proceeded on leave.	
	31st			

[signatures]

14.

50 Mob. Vet. Sect. 39 D.M.S. 5??

Army Form C. 2118.

WAR DIARY
or
INTELLIGENCE SUMMARY.

(Erase heading not required.)

February 1918

Vol 24

Place	Date	Hour	Summary of Events and Information	Remarks and references to Appendices
Morcourt	1/2/6		No 25631 Pte Myatt H.E. proceeded on leave.	
"	2nd		No 3500 and No 9598 Pte's Baylis and Green proceeded on leave.	
"	2nd		Moved from MORCOURT to NURLU	
NURLU	3rd		Prepared animals for evacuation	
"	4th		Evacuated 6 Horses and 6 Mules to VII Corps M.V.D.	
"	5th		Evacuated 1 Horse to VII Corps M.V.D. Visited 14 labour Coy 57th A.T. Coy R.E. & 178 Tunnelling Coy	
"	6th		Sector Raid. 1 N.C.O and Bn??? sent for VII Corps M.V.D. Visited 132/133 Field Amb & 227 Coy R.E.	
"	7th		Evacuated 17 Horses 2 Mules to VII Corps M.V.D.	
"	8th		Kit Parade. Visited 14 labour Coy 57th A.T. Coy R.E. 178 Tunnelling Coy and 132 Field Amb & 227 Field Coy R.E.	
"	9th		Prepared animals for evacuation	
"	10th		Evacuated 26 Horses & 6 Mules to VII Corps M.V.D.	
"	11th		237 Pte Pinto?? proceeded on leave & No 27015 Pte Rother H. joined from No 2 Vet Hospital.	
"	12th		No 12722 Pte G.E. Brown proceeded to No 2 Veterinary Hospital for examination as A.V.C. B.S. Sgt.	
"	13th		Visited 14 labour Coy, 57th A.T. Coy R.E. & 176 Tunnelling Coy.	
"	14th		Evacuated 20 Horses and 5 Mules to VII Corps M.V.D. Pte Gill A.C. (236 Emp Coy) proceeded on leave.	
"	15th		1 Mn?? despatched to ABBEVILLE for Glanders?? Visited 132, 133 Field Amb and 227 Field Coy R.E.	

Army Form C. 2118.

WAR DIARY
or
INTELLIGENCE SUMMARY.
(Erase heading not required.)

Instructions regarding War Diaries and Intelligence Summaries are contained in F. S. Regs., Part II. and the Staff Manual respectively. Title pages will be prepared in manuscript.

February 1918.

Place	Date	Hour	Summary of Events and Information	Remarks and references to Appendices
Nurlu	16th		Visited 132 Field Ambulance, 133 F Amb, and 227th Field Coy R.E.	
"	17th		No.25031 Pte Allgarott R.E. returned off leave. Visited 1st Labour Coy, 57th A.T. Coy R.E & 178 Tunnelling Coy.	
"	18th		Evacuated 18 Horses and 9 Mules. 2 Cast animals. To VII Corps at J.17. No 137949 Pte Pyles T.N. proceeded on leave.	
"	20th		No 3500 Pte Rayle a & No 9598 Pte Green N.7. returned from leave.	
"	21st		Evacuated 13 Horses, 7 Mules and 1 Cast animal to VII Corps at J.17	
"	22nd		Section Red Rifle Drill. Visited 132, 133 Field Amb. and 227 Field Coy R.E.	
"	23rd		Section Red Rifle Drill.	
"	25th		Evacuated 16 Horses and Mules to VII Corps at J.17. Visited 114 Labour Coy, 574 A.T. Coy R.E and 178 Tunnelling Coy.	
"	27th		Section Red Rifle Drill	
"	28th		Evacuated 18 Horses, 1 Mule and 1 Cast animal to VII Corps at J.17. Section Raid	
"			Visited 132, 133 Field Ambulance and 227 Field Coy R.E.	

Dickson Captain
Comdg 50th M.V.S.

Army Form C. 2118.

50 Meth. V.B. See 39

March 1916

WAR DIARY
or
INTELLIGENCE SUMMARY

(Erase heading not required.)

Instructions regarding War Diaries and Intelligence Summaries are contained in F. S. Regs., Part II. and the Staff Manual respectively. Title Pages will be prepared in manuscript.

Place	Date	Hour	Summary of Events and Information	Remarks and references to Appendices
Neulu	1st		Visited 227th. Coy R.E. & 132, 133, Field Ambulances	
"	2nd		Rd Point returned off leave.	
"	3rd		" Wegn's proceeded on leave.	
"	4th		Evacuated 11 Horses + 1 Mule to 38th M.V.S.	
"	5th		Visited 133 Field Ambulance	
"	6th		Visited 1st Labour Coy, 674 A.T. Coy R.E. 16s Labour Coy, 176 mm. Coy & 72 Labour Coy.	
"	7th		Evac. 23 Horses & 6 Mules to 33rd M.V.S.	
"	8th		Visited 133 Field Ambulance	
"	9th		Pte Inglis returned off leave	
"	10th		Evac: 33 Horses + 4 Mules + 2 Goat animals to 33rd M.V.S.	
"	11th		Evac 7 Horses to 33rd M.V.S. Moved to Foret d'Ecrin's	
"	12th			
Foret d'Ecrin's	13th		Visited 135 Field Ambulance	
"	14th		Evacuated 7 Horses to 33rd M.V.S.	
"	15th		Evac. 1 Horse " " "	
"	16th		Visited 133 Field Ambulance	
"	18th		Evacuated 16 Horses, 1 Mule, & 2 Goat mules to 33 M.V.S.). Visited 133th Ambulance	
"	20th		1 Mule sent to VII Corps V.E.S. Capt Shelton proceeded on leave. Major Sames D.A.D.V.S. 39th Division took over command of Unit.	

WAR DIARY
or
INTELLIGENCE SUMMARY

Army Form C. 2118.

(Erase heading not required.)

2nd ---- March 1916

Place	Date	Hour	Summary of Events and Information	Remarks and references to Appendices
	22nd		Moved from East Allains to Blay	
	23rd		" Blay to Morieux and then to Coffy.	
	24th		" Coffy to Bluignolles	
	25th		" Bluignolles to Corrier	
	26th		" Corrier to outskirts of Corbie	
	27th		" Outskirts of Corbie to Gratchets of Blangy-Tronville	
	29th		" Gratchets of Blangy-Tronville to Gratchets of Bove's.	
	30th		" Bove's to St Maween	

This Unit arrived in France on 6/3/16.

[Signature] Barnes
Major D.A.D.V.S.
for O.C. 50th M.V.S.

No. 14

50 Mob Vety Sec 39
Army Form C. 2118.

WAR DIARY
or
INTELLIGENCE SUMMARY.
(Erase heading not required.)

Instructions regarding War Diaries and Intelligence Summaries are contained in F. S. Regs., Part II. and the Staff Manual respectively. Title pages will be prepared in manuscript.

April 1918

YA 26

Place	Date	Hour	Summary of Events and Information	Remarks and references to Appendices
	1st		Moved from St Musien to Guyencourt	
	2nd		Moved from Guyencourt to Forney	
	3rd		Moved from Forney to Andainville	
Andainville	6th		Visited 29= D.H.S. Evac: 14 Horses & 2 Mules to 14 Vet. Hospital Abbeville	
	7th		Moved from Andainville to Gamaches	
Gamaches	8th		Visited D.D.V.S.	
	9th		Moved from Gamaches to Eu, and entrained to Argues.	
Argues	10th		Capt Skelton returned off leave and resumed duties as O.C. 50 M.I.S.	
	11th		Moved from Argues to Eperlecques - Estrant. Pte Wegus returned off leave.	
Eperlecques-Estrant	12th		Evac: 1 Horse to 23 Veterinary Hospital St Omer Visited 132 Field Ambulance	
"	13th		Evac. 2 Horses & 2 Mules to 23 Vet. Hospital St Omer. No 11834 Pte Todd F.H.T. despatched to No 2 Vet Hospital	
"	14th		Visited 132, 133 & 134 Field Ambulance	
"	15th		Evac. 3 Horses to 23 Veterinary Hospital St Omer	
"	16th			
"	17th		Visited 132, 133 & 134 Field Ambulance	
"	18th		Evac. 2 Horses & 2 Mules to 23 Veterinary Hospital St Omer	
"	19th		Visited Ax? Calin: Section had Drill Visited 132 Field Ambulance	
"	20th		Sister Paid	
"	21st			

A6945. Wt. W14422/M1160. 350,000 12/16. D. D. & L. Forms/C/2118/14.

Army Form C. 2118.

WAR DIARY
or
INTELLIGENCE SUMMARY. April 1916
(Erase heading not required.)

Place	Date	Hour	Summary of Events and Information	Remarks and references to Appendices
Etaples-Etaput	22ⁿᵈ		Evac. 2 horses to 23 Veterinary Hospital. Section Rod Rifle Inspection + Drill	
	23ʳᵈ		Visited 132 Field Ambulance.	
	24ᵗʰ		Visited 138 & 134 Field Ambulances. Section Rod Drill.	
	25ᵗʰ		Evac. 1 Mule + 1 Cart Mule to 23 Veterinary Hospital. Visited 132 Field Ambulance.	
	26ᵗʰ		No 20663 Pte. Kaye G.H. A.V.C. joined from No 2 Vet. Hospital to complete establishment	
			Visited 132, 133 & 134 Field Ambulance.	
	28ᵗʰ		Section Rod Drill.	
	29ᵗʰ		Visited Field Cashier. Section Rod Rifle Inspection. Visited 132 Field Ambulance.	
	30ᵗʰ		Section Rod. Visited 132 Field Ambulance.	

Unit formed in October 1915.
Date of embarkation for France. 6/3/16.

Cullen
Captain
Cmdg 50 C.V.S.

50th Mobile Vety Section

WAR DIARY
INTELLIGENCE SUMMARY.
(Erase heading not required.)

May 1915

Place	Date	Hour	Summary of Events and Information	Remarks and references to Appendices
Ebblinghem	1st		Evacuated 1 Horse to 23rd Vety Hospital St Omer.	
"	2nd		Visited 133 and 134 Field Ambulance	
"	3rd		Evacuated 1 Horse to 23rd Vet Hospital St Omer. Visited 132 Field Ambulance.	
"	4th		Evacuated 3 Horses to 23rd Vet Hospital St Omer	
"	5th		Visited 133 and 134 Field Ambulance	
"	6th		Visited 132 Field Ambulance	
"	7th		No 27015 Pte Rattey F. A.V.C. Evacuated Sick	
"	8th		Visited 132, 133 and 134 Field Ambulance	
"	9th		Evacuated 4 Horses and 2 Mules to 23rd Veterinary Hospital St Omer.	
"	10th		Visited 132 Field Ambulance	
"	11th		Visited 133 and 134 Field Ambulance	
"	12th		Evacuated 4 Horses to 23rd Vet Hospital St Omer	
"	13th		Evacuated 1 Colt to No 5 Base Remount Depot Calais. Visited 133 Field Ambulance	
"	14th		Evacuated 7 Horses to 23rd Vet Hospital St Omer. Visited 132 Field Ambulance. Section Raid.	
"	15th		Evacuated 5 Horses to 23rd Vet Hospital St Omer. Assumed duties of A/D.A.D.V.S. whilst absent Somer	
"	16th		D.A.D.V.S. 39th Divs: on leave.	

X Mobile formed September 1915. X
X Date of Embarkation for France 5/3/16 X

Army Form C. 2118.

50 - Mobile Vet Section.
WAR DIARY
or
INTELLIGENCE SUMMARY.
(Erase heading not required.)

May 1918

Instructions regarding War Diaries and Intelligence Summaries are contained in F.S. Regs., Part II. and the Staff Manual respectively. Title pages will be prepared in manuscript.

Place	Date	Hour	Summary of Events and Information	Remarks and references to Appendices
Etaples	19th		Visited 16 Cheshire Regt and 39th Signals R.E.	
"	20th		Unit attended Baths	
"	21st		Evacuated 3 Horses to 23rd Vet Hospital St Omer. Visited Chief Veterinarian 77th American Division.	
"	23rd		Evacuated 3 Horses to 23rd Vet Hospital St Omer. Visited Horses Corrals. Visited 1st Canadian Res. Park.	
"			Visited S Sect 2nd Army Aux Horse Transport, also H Sect, H.Q. and part of I Sect. 2nd Army Aux Hse Trspt	
"	24		Section Raid.	
"	25		Evacuated 6 Horses to 23rd Vet Hospital St Omer.	
"	26		Visited Chief Veterinarian 77th American Division.	
"	27		Visited Chinese Labour Corp and 15th Reserve Park. Also visited Units situated at Tournehem, Bonningues, Andres, and Welles-bay-Orderes, and visited Bonningues again in the evening.	
"	28		Evacuated 7 Horses + Mules to 23rd Vet Hospital St Omer. Lectured and gave demonstrations to H.Q. Veterinary Officer of 117th American Division	
"	29		Inspected animals being landed and by the following Units:- 11 and 13th R Sussex Regt, 17th K.R.R.C., 16th Rifle Brigade and 13th Gloucester Regt, to 30th American Division.	
"	30		Evacuated 4 Horses to 23rd Vet Hospital St Omer. Visited 225th Field Coy R.E., 5 Sect 2nd Army Aux Horse Transport + Chanson Park	
"	31st		Visited Chief Veterinarian 77th American Division, and visited 3rd Fw H.T. and outlying Units.	

Captain C.
Cmdg 50th Mob. Vet. Sect.

WAR DIARY
or
INTELLIGENCE SUMMARY.
(Erase heading not required.)

Army Form C. 2118.

50 Mob. Vet. Secn
June 1918

Vol 28

Place	Date	Hour	Summary of Events and Information	Remarks and references to Appendices
Eperlecques	1st		Evacuated 2 Horses to 23 Veterinary Hospital St. Omer. No 589 Staff-Sergt Smith H. deg/attd	
			to No 2 H. Veterinary Hospital for duty. Daily Routine work.	
"	2nd		H. officer deg/attd to No 2 Veterinary Hospital ? supplies to Establishment.	
"	3rd		Visited 3 Sect. 1st Canadian Res. Park, "G" Coy Sqr. 2nd Indian and 30th American D.H.Q. Daily Routine work	
"	4th		Visited No 5 Sect No 2 Army Aux. Horse Transport Coy. Daily Routine work.	
"	5th		Evacuated 19 Horses to 23 Veterinary Hospital St Omer. Daily Routine work.	
"	6th		Evacuated 3 Horses to 23 Veterinary Hospital St Omer. Daily Routine work.	
"	7th		Evacuated 2 Horses to 23 Veterinary Hospital St Omer. Daily Routine work.	
"			Moved to Rodelinghem. Daily routine work	
Rodelinghem	8th		Daily Routine work	
"	9th		Evacuated 1 Horse a lettuce to the Australian Vet Hospital CALAIS. Daily Routine work.	
"	10th		Collected Horse from LIGNES. Daily Routine work.	
"	11th		Evacuated 1 Horse to the Australian Vet Hospital CALAIS. Daily Routine work.	
"			Visited H Sect. No 14 Army Aux. H.T. Coy, 9 Black Watch, and NIELLES-LES-ARDRES.	
"	12th		Evacuated 1 Horse to No 19 Veterinary Hospital CALAIS. Visited 7 Gordons, No 10 Gordons,	
			and 6th Argyle & Suth Highlanders. Daily Routine work. Visited ? General billet at ATHINGUES	

Army Form C. 2118.

WAR DIARY
or
INTELLIGENCE SUMMARY.
(Erase heading not required.)

June 1918

Place	Date	Hour	Summary of Events and Information	Remarks and references to Appendices
Ruddingham	13		Daily Routine work.	
"	14		Moved to AUTINGUES. Daily Routine work.	
Autingues	15		Float proceeded to HENNEVEUX to collect horse. A.N.C.O. proceeded to LICQUES to collect horse. Daily Routine work.	
"	16		Float proceeded to RUMMINGHEM to collect horse. Daily Routine work.	
"	17		Evacuated 5 Horses and 1 Mule to the Australian Vet Hospital CALAIS.	
"			Visited 225 Field Coy R.E. Daily Routine work.	
"	18		Evacuated 13 Horses to Australian Vet. Hospital CALAIS. Visited No.4 Army Aux. H.T. Coy.	
"			Daily Routine work.	
"	19		Visited No.4 Coy. 39th Div. Train and Chief Veterinarian H.D. 60 Inf. Bde. 30th American Division. Daily Routine work.	
"	20		Evacuated 5 Horses to the Australian Vet Hospital CALAIS. Visited Field Bakery, and handed over animals to 115 M.G.C. (30 American Division) Daily Routine work.	
"			Section Rivet.	
"	21		Evacuated 9 Horses and 1 Mule to the Australian Veterinary Hospital. Daily Routine work.	

WAR DIARY or INTELLIGENCE SUMMARY.

Army Form C. 2118.

June 1918.

Place	Date	Hour	Summary of Events and Information	Remarks and references to Appendices
Motinque	August 22nd		Evacuated 2 Horses to Australian Vet. Hospital CALAIS. Handed over animals at	
"	23rd		Northorpe to 105 Signal Coy. 30 American Division. Visited D.A.D.V.S. 34	
"			Division H.S. Daily Routine work.	
"	24th		Evacuated 2 Horses to Australian Vet. Hospital. Daily Routine work.	
"	25th		Daily Routine work.	
"			Daily Routine work.	
"	26th		Evacuated 2 Horses and 1 Remount to Australian Vet. Hospital. Visited 225 Field Coy.R.E.	
"			Daily Routine work.	
"	27th		Evacuated 1 Horse to the Australian Vet Hospital CALAIS. Daily Routine work.	
"	28th		Daily Routine work	
"	29th		Visited No H Sect No 4 Army Aux. H.T.Coy. Daily Routine work.	
"	30th		Evacuated 11 Horses to the Australian Vet Hospital CALAIS. Daily Routine work	

Cochrane C.
Officer Cmdg 30 Cy.V.S.

50th Mobile Vety Section

Army Form C. 2118.

WAR DIARY
or
INTELLIGENCE SUMMARY.

July 1918.   Vol 29

Place	Date	Hour	Summary of Events and Information	Remarks and references to Appendices
Ostrohove	1st		Daily Routine Work.	
"	2nd		Evacuated 5 Horses to Australian Vety Hospital CALAIS. Visited No 4 S.T. No 4 Army Aux H.T.Q. and H Coy 39 Div Train. L.H. 8 and Steel Rawlind. No 11503 Pte Hakes C.S. Congratulated to No 5 Veterinary Hospital. Daily Routine Work.	
"	3rd		Visited 132nd 133rd Field Ambulances and 225th Field Coy R.E. Daily Routine Work.	
"	4th		Section Paid. Evacuated 5 Horses to Australian Vet Hospital CALAIS. Visited 13 Gloucester Regt. Daily Routine Work.	
"	5th		No 5 H Coy 39 Div Train and 112 Field Ambulance. Daily Routine Work.	
"	6th		Daily Routine Work.	
"	7th		Visited 112th H.3rd Field Ambulances. Daily Routine Work.	
"	8th		Evacuated 1 Horse to Aux S. Veterinary Hospital CALAIS. 9503 Pte Hawkens W.R.	
"	9th		Proceeded on Leave. Daily Routine Work.	
"	10th		Daily Routine Work.	
"	9th		Visited No 4 S.T. No 4 Army Aux H.T.Q. Daily Routine Work.	
"	10th		Evacuated 4 Horses to Aus. Vet Hospital CALAIS. Visited 112 Field Ambulance + 28th Northumberland Fusiliers. Daily Routine Work.	
"	11th		Float sent to POLINCOVE to collect animal. Visited No 4 Coy 39 Div Train	

Army Form C. 2118.

50 L Mobile Vety Section

WAR DIARY
or
INTELLIGENCE SUMMARY.
(Erase heading not required.)

July 1918

Place	Date	Hour	Summary of Events and Information	Remarks and references to Appendices
Anticques	11		Visited 225 Field Coy. R.E., 1/25 + 1/24 London Regts. Daily Routine work.	
"	12		Evacuated 3 Horses to Australian Vet Hospital CALAIS. Section paraded for tasks. Daily Routine work.	
"	13		Unit Moved to LICQUES. Visited Area Commandant Licques. Daily Routine work.	
LICQUES	14		Daily Routine work.	
"	15		Visited 112 Field Ambulance. Daily Routine Work.	
"	16		Visited Area Commandant Licques. Daily Routine work	
"	17		Visited 225 Field Coy. R.E., 13 Gloucester Regt. 112 Field Ambulance. No 4 Coy. 39 Div. Train. Daily Routine work.	
"	18		Evacuated 6 Horses to Australian Vet Hospital CALAIS, Visited 112 Field Ambulance. Collected Rose from "E" W.A.S.T. Daily Routine work.	
"	19		Visited "F" wheeling Gun Btn. to inspect animals but unit had not arrived. Float.	
"	20		Proceeded to "E" W.A.S.T. to collect animal. Daily Routine work.	
"	21		Evacuated 5 Horses to Australian Vet. Hospital CALAIS. Daily Routine work.	
"	22		Visited Field Cashier 39 D.H.Q. Section Paid. Daily Routine work.	

50ᵗʰ Mobile Vet. Section

WAR DIARY
or
INTELLIGENCE SUMMARY.

(Erase heading not required.)

July 1918

Place	Date	Hour	Summary of Events and Information	Remarks and references to Appendices
Fiefs	23rd		Visited 112 Field Ambulances and "F" Machine Gun. Bn. Daily Routine Work.	
"	24th		Visited No H Coy 39 Div. Train 13 L Gloucester Regt and 225 Field Coy R.E.	
"	25th		Daily Routine Work.	
"			Unit moved to Antenguin's. Daily Routine Work.	
Antenguin's	26th		Evacuated 2 horses and 1 mule (Hot Remounts) to Australian Vet Hospital Calais.	
"			Daily Routine Work.	
"	27th		Visited 39 T.M.B. Daily Routine Work.	
"	28th		M9503 Pte Hawkins w.R. returned off leave. Daily Routine Work.	
"	29th		Unit proceeded to 112 Field Ambulance. Enquire's for animal. Resting. Proceeded to LR Inspection Section. Proceeded to Boll. Daily Routine Work.	Vehicle No 14 Coy 39 Div Train
"	30th		Visited "F" Machine Gun. Bn. and Mallonial animals. Daily Routine Work.	
"	31st		Visited 112 Field Amb. and 225 Field Coy R.E. and "F" Machine Gun Bn.	
"			Daily Routine Work. Unit proceeded to Bolembert for Renewal	

Signatures

Capt. A.V.C.
Officer Comdg 50 L.M.V.S.

WAR DIARY or **INTELLIGENCE SUMMARY**

Army Form C. 2118.

50 Two Vetinsee 39
VII CORPS.

50 - Mobile Veterinary Section

August 1916.

Place	Date	Hour	Summary of Events and Information	Remarks and references to Appendices
Aubigny	1		Evacuated 2 Horses totals to Australian Veterinary Hospital Calais. Visited 13th Gloucester Regt and No 4 Coy 39th Tal Train. Daily Routine work.	
"	2		Daily routine work.	
"	3		Evacuated 1 Horse to Australian Veterinary Hospital Calais. Visited Field Railway Section Ravel. Daily Routine work.	
"	4		Daily routine work.	
"	5		Visited 225 Field Coy R.E. Daily routine work.	
"	6		Meat Inspected. To Observers for animals. Visited 39th Divl T.R. Daily routine work.	
"	7		Evacuated 1 Horse and 2 Mules to Australian Veterinary Hospital Calais. Visited H et 9 Bn 116th Brigade H.Q. 225 Field Coy R.E. - Battn. Lorries. Daily Routine work.	
"	8		Evacuated 1 Horse to Australian Veterinary Hospital. Visited 13th Gloucester Regt No 4 Coy 39th Tal Train. Daily Routine work	
"	9		Evacuated 1 Horse and 2 Mules to Australian Vety Hospital. Visited 2nd Field Coy R.E. Daily Routine work	
"	10		Visited 13th Gloucester Regt. No 4 Sect No 4 Army Aux Horse Transport Coy. Daily Routine work.	
"	11		Evacuated 4 Horses and 1 Mule to Australian Veterinary Hospital. Daily Routine work.	
"	12		Pt's Good and Owen. A.V.C. proceeded to No 16 Veterinary Hospital Calais for course of training rifle nm. Visited No 4 Sect No 4 Army Aux H.T.C. 225 Field Coy R.E.	

Army Form C. 2118.

WAR DIARY
or
INTELLIGENCE SUMMARY

(Erase heading not required.)

50th Mobile Veterinary August 1916.

Instructions regarding War Diaries and Intelligence Summaries are contained in F. S. Regs., Part II. and the Staff Manual respectively. Title Pages will be prepared in manuscript.

Place	Date	Hour	Summary of Events and Information	Remarks and references to Appendices
Antigues	12		Section had musketry drill. Daily routine work.	
	13		Evacuated 1 Horse to Australian Vety Hospital. Visited Fresh Chalive. Pt's Ruest and Williams A.V.C. joined from No 2 Con Horse Depot. Daily Routine work.	
	14		Ofr's Purves and Carey went to No 2 Veterinary Hospital for examination. Evacuated 1 Horse to Australian Vety Hospital Chalon. Daily Routine work. Sectn Pard	
	15		Captain Skeete R.T.A.V.C evacuated sick	
	16		Sectn proceeded to "E" at 9½ km for animal. Capt'n Smyth R.A.V.C. reassumed temporary command.	
	17		Daily routine work. Moved to Lumbres	
Lumbres	18		Evacuated 6 Horses to 23 Veterinary Hospital St Omer. Daily routine work.	
	19		Capt'n Broadhurst O.f.S. A.V.C. reassumed temporary command.	
			Visited unit at last. Daily Routine work.	
	20		Evacuated 2 Horses to 23 Vety Hospital St Omer. Captain Skeeny W.A.V.C. resumed command. Section held Kit, Saddle and Rifle inspection.	
			Daily Routine work.	

WAR DIARY or INTELLIGENCE SUMMARY

Army Form C. 2118.

No. 3

No. 50 Mobile Veterinary Section   August 1916

Place	Date	Hour	Summary of Events and Information	Remarks and references to Appendices
Fumbres	21st		Visited No 1 Canadian B.A.H.T.C. - Daily Routine work.	
"	22nd		Visited 285, 286 and 287 Coys A.S.C. and 573 (Cornwall) A.T.R.E. Daily Routine work.	
"	23rd		Daily Routine work.	
"	24th		Mounted Drill. Capt? Broadhurst O.S. A.V.C. proceeded to report to D.A.D.V.S. 49th Divn.	
"	25th		Daily Routine work. Mounted Drill and exercise.	
"	26th		Evacuated 1 Horse to No 23 Veterinary Hospital St Omer. Daily Routine work.	
"	27th		Mounted Drill and exercise. Visited South African Mhets. Daily Routine work.	
"	28th		Mounted Drill and exercise. Inspected site for new camp at Sercette, but found it unsatisfactory. Daily Routine work.	
"	29th		Visited No 1 Can. B.A.H.T.C. 285, 286 and 287 Coys A.S.C. and 573 (Cornwall) A.T.R.E. Daily Routine work.	
"	30th		Mounted Drill. Visited 573 (Cornwall) A.T.R.E. Prepared new camp. Daily Routine work.	
"	31st		Mounted Drill and exercise. Battery formed. Daily Routine work.	

W. Whiteley Capt. A.V.C.
O/C 50 M.V.S.

Army Form C. 2118.

WAR DIARY
or
INTELLIGENCE SUMMARY

(Erase heading not required.)

50 Mtd Vety Sec September 1918

Place	Date	Hour	Summary of Events and Information	Remarks and references to Appendices
Lindres	1st		Mounted drill and exercise. Daily routine work	
	2nd		Mounted drill and exercise. Checks Sgt Officer from 513 Bomb'd RE	
			285, 286, 287 bay ASC. Off Bowes agent from N°2 Vety Hospital	
	3rd		Mounted drill and exercise. Horses Op 1 Bomb'd ADHTC Lindres 41	
	4th		Loose 2 horses and 1 mule to N° 23 Vet Hospital Rouen 53	
			Mounted drill and exercise. Checks from Lemaire Fournier and the	
			Bn HQ, 2nd Regt Scots Inf, 9 Regt Rifle SAH	
			Ion bay 1st S'oft African Inf by 2nd and 4th Scot Gycos	
			9th MacD Ambs by 513 Bomb RE 285 286 287 bays SE	
			Ad. N°1 Bomb'd ADHTC & 102 Engineers 27 borrow kitbag	
	5th		Mounted drill and exercise. Daily routine work	
	6th		Checks Off Canning AAHTC. Mounted drill and exer	
	7th		Forwards 1 horse to N° 23 Vety Hospice Rouen and 1wol	
			Checks Lieut Crocker and ADVS HQ VII Corps Scott Plant	
			Mounted drill and exercise. Park canty work	
	8th		Mounted drill and exercise. Daily routine work	

Army Form C. 2118.

WAR DIARY
or
INTELLIGENCE SUMMARY.
(Erase heading not required.)

Instructions regarding War Diaries and Intelligence Summaries are contained in F. S. Regs., Part II. and the Staff Manual respectively. Title pages will be prepared in manuscript.

2

So. Mob. Vet. September 1918

Place	Date	Hour	Summary of Events and Information	Remarks and references to Appendices
Aube	9		Marched thirst and seven only rendervous with	
"	10		Moved to No 23 Veterinary Hospital for duty	
St Omer	11		Daily routine work	
"	12		Daily routine work	
"	13		Lt Whitear evacuated sick to Hopkins D.G.V.S. inspected horses	
"	14		Daily routine work	
"	15		Capt Swift from No 23 Vet Hospital posted to take	
			Lt Whiteas vacancy Capt K.R. Swift reported for duty	
"	16		Rd received orders from No 2 Vet Hospital to be held in readiness with	
"	17		Lt Swift posted to D.D.V.S. 2nd ARMY for duty Exercising & Grazing continued	
"	18		Lt Reynolds promoted to No 2 duty hospital in command pending of promotion	
			to rank of A.V.C. Sergeant to a field unit. Daily routine with	
"	19		Daily routine work and exercise	
"	20		Daily routine work and exercise	
"	21		Laid section evacuated horses to Calais	
"	22		Daily routine work and exercise.	

Army Form C. 2118.

WAR DIARY
or
INTELLIGENCE SUMMARY

(Erase heading not required.)

55 Mob Veterinary Section   September 1918.

Instructions regarding War Diaries and Intelligence Summaries are contained in F.S. Regs., Part II. and the Staff Manual respectively. Title Pages will be prepared in manuscript.

Place	Date	Hour	Summary of Events and Information	Remarks and references to Appendices
St Omer	23		Generated horse to Intinghem. Only routine work and exercise	
	24		Generated horse to Intinghem. Daily routine work and exercise	
	25		Generated horse to Intinghem. Daily routine work and exercise	
	26		Sent proceeded to Blanck Sh. HQ. Case Card routine work and exercise	
	27		Generated horse to Anvin Road. Daily routine work and exercise	
	28		Moved to Audruicq	
	29		Moved to STAPLE and took over Days head	
	30		Daily routine work	

W Shipley Capt RVC
Comdg 55 Mobile Veterinary Section

50 Mob Vety Sec
October 1918 Vol 3

1. WAR DIARY
or
INTELLIGENCE SUMMARY.

Army Form C. 2118.

50th Mobile Veterinary Section

Place	Date	Hour	Summary of Events and Information	Remarks and references to Appendices
STAVELE	1.		Evacuated 72 animals to 23rd Veterinary Hospital by lorry. Daily routine work.	
	2.		Moved to ELVERDINGHE. Evacuated 23 animals to No. 8. V.E.S. Daily routine work.	
	3		Evacuated 20 animals (1 stat case) to No. 8. V.E.S. Routine work. Visited Corps H.Q.	
	4.		Evacuated 25 animals (1 stat case) to No. 8. V.E.S. Daily routine work	
	5.		Evacuated 19 animals (3 stat cases) to No. 8 V.E.S Daily routine work. Visited Corps H.Q.	
	6.		Evacuated 47 animals (2 stat cases) to No. 8. V.E.S. The Colonel commanded to Hospitals.	
			Daily routine work	
	7.		Evacuated 22 animals (4 stat cases). 2 horses destroyed and buried. Visited	
			Field Cashier. Daily routine work.	
	8.		Section Paid. Evacuated 30 animals (3 stat cases) Daily routine work.	
	9.		Evacuated 24 animals (2 stat cases) Daily routine work.	
	10.		Evacuated 18 animals (3 stat cases) to No. 8 V.E.S. Lt. Robinson J. proceeded	
			on leave. Daily routine work. 1 horse destroyed and buried.	
	11.		Evacuated 29 animals (2 stat cases) to No. 8 V.E.S Daily routine work	
	12.		Evacuated 8 animals (3 stat cases) to No. 8 V.E.S Daily routine work	
	13.		Evacuated 7 animals to No. 2 V.E.S. Visited 21st Mob. Vet. Sect. and	
			went of taking over their lines. Daily routine work.	
	14.		Evacuated 11 animals (1 stat case) and 1 horse to No. 2. V.E.S Daily Routine work	

Army Form C. 2118.

WAR DIARY or INTELLIGENCE SUMMARY

(Erase heading not required.)

50 Mobile Veterinary Section **Oct 1918**

Place	Date	Hour	Summary of Events and Information	Remarks and references to Appendices
Potijze	15.		Moved to Potijze. Mobile hosp. H.Q. Evacuated 29 animals (2 Horse cars) to N° 2 V.E.S. Daily routine work	
"	16.		Visited Zonnebeke to make arrangements for new lines. One N.C.O and 2 men proceeded to Zonnebeke to make them standing. 3 men lines. Evacuated 3 animals (3 Horse cars) to N° 2 V.E.S. Daily routine work.	
"	17.		Moved to Zonnebeke. Evacuated 41 animals (2 Horse cars) to N° 2 V.E.S. Daily routine work.	
"	18.		Visited St Pieter to make arrangements for new lines. Evacuated 16 animals to N° 2 V.E.S. Daily routine work.	
"	19.		Moved to St Pieter. One horse destroyed and buried. Daily routine work. Admitted 18 animals	
"	20.		One horse destroyed and buried. Daily routine work. Admitted 37 animals	
"	21.		One horse destroyed and buried. Daily routine work. Admitted 10 animals	
LENDELEDE	22.		Evacuated 62 animals to N° 2 V.E.S. Moved near Lendelede. Daily routine work	
"	23.		Evacuated 29 animals (2 Horse cars) 18" and 21" Mob. Vet. Sections to N° 2 V.E.S. Pte Carr. proceeded on leave. Daily routine work	

Army Form C. 2118.

3 WAR DIARY
or
INTELLIGENCE SUMMARY.
(Erase heading not required.)

50th Mobile Veterinary Section   October 1918

Place	Date	Hour	Summary of Events and Information	Remarks and references to Appendices
Auchel	24		Evacuated 22 animals to No 2 V.E.S. Cut three destroyed and buried. Arranging new pils for No 2 V.E.S.	
"	25		Evacuated 30 animals (1 Horse case) to No 2 V.E.S. Daily routine work.	
"	26		Evacuated 16 animals (1 Horse case) to No 2 V.E.S. Arranged new release for Section. Pte Simpson proceeded on leave. Daily routine work.	
"	27		Evacuated 18 animals to No 2 V.E.S. Arranged new pils at HEULLE for No 2 V.E.S. Pte Robinson reported from leave. Daily routine work. Visited Attestion at Condicin	
"	28		Evacuated 28 animals (1 Horse float and 2 Water float) Daily routine work.	
"	29		Evacuated 7 animals (1 Horse float) to No 2 V.E.S. Two horses (Battle cases) conveyed by Horse float to Attestion Condicin. Visited Corps H.Q.	
"	30		Worked to Chart to arrange lines for Section. Moved to Chart.	
"	31		Cor Wheels conveyed by float to Attestion Condicin. Daily routine work.	

W. H. Hany Capt. A.V.C.
Comdg 50th Mob. Vet. Sect

A 5834 Wt. W4973/M687 750,000 8/16 D. D. & L. Ltd. Forms/C.2118/13.

To
D A G
G.H.Q 3rd Echelon

Herewith War Diary for
the month of November 1918
of the Section under my
Command please

W Shipley Captain
Comdg 50 Mob Vet Sect

Army Form C. 2118.

50 M.U.T

WAR DIARY
or
INTELLIGENCE SUMMARY.
(Erase heading not required.)

50 Mobile Veterinary Section

November 1918

No C 3

Place	Date	Hour	Summary of Events and Information	Remarks and references to Appendices
Le Chat.	1.		Arrived 1 animal Evacuated 1 animal to No 2 V.E.S. Visited II Corps H.Q. and Sup Barters. Daily routine work	
"	2.		Section Parade. Daily routine work	
"	3.		Admitted 3 animals. Visited II Corps H.Q. Daily routine work	
"	4.		Admitted 1 animal. Evac. 1 animal to No 2 V.E.S. 1/6 S.H. reported for duty	
"	5.		Daily routine work	
"	6.		Daily routine work	
"	7.		Admitted 2 animals. Daily routine work	
"	8.		Evacuated 2 animals to No 2 V.E.S. Daily routine work. Visited Launa to make arrangements to meet Section. Visited II Corps H.Q.	
LAUWE	9.		Moved to Launa. Admitted 4 animals. Daily routine work	
"	10.		Daily routine work	
"	11.		Evacuated 4 animals to No 2 V.E.S. Visited II Corps H.Q. Daily routine work	
"	12.		Admitted 2 animals. Visited II Corps H.Q. Daily routine work	
"	13.		Evacuated 2 animals to No 2 V.E.S. Dr Daley proceeded on leave. Daily routine work	
"	14.		Visited II Corps H.Q. and Sup. Barters. Per Simpson returned from leave. Daily routine work	

Army Form C. 2118.

WAR DIARY
or
INTELLIGENCE SUMMARY.

(Erase heading not required.)

50th Mobile Vet Sec.   November 1918

Place	Date	Hour	Summary of Events and Information	Remarks and references to Appendices
LAVVE	14		Sick and Casual 1 animal, also 1 died, also treated 2 shoes	
	15		Daily routine work	
	16		Visited XIX Corps HQ. Daily routine work	
	17		Admitted 1 animal Casual, 1 animal (sick case) 2 N.I.C.V.F.S. Daily routine work	
	18		Daily routine work	
	19		Admitted 1 animal. Daily routine work	
	20		Daily routine work	
	21		Went to DEERLYCK. Daily routine work	
	22		Went to Police. Barracks and moved to N° 45 Mob Vet Sect. Daily routine work	
	23		Went to St Sylvester Barracks. Daily routine work	
	24		Went to N° 23 Veterinary Hospital St Omer (Tatinghem)	
Tatinghem	25		Daily routine work. Visited Lees Barbul	
	26		Section and Sick take over and Daily routine work	
	27		Opt Swan reported for duty. Daily routine work	
	28		Visited N° 23 Veterinary Hospital and Transport Service Inspection work	
	29		Daily routine work. Visited N° 23 Veterinary Hospital and Transport	

Army Form C. 2118.

WAR DIARY
or
INTELLIGENCE SUMMARY.

(Erase heading not required.)

Title pages 50 Mobile Vet Sec

Place	Date	Hour	Summary of Events and Information	Remarks and references to Appendices
Valcartier	30		Moved Nº 23 Veterinary Hospital and transport. Only routine work.	
			Luttlejohns Capt AVC	
			Comdg 50 Mobile Veterinary Section	

1

To DAG.
G.H.Q 3rd Echelon

Herewith War Diary for
the month of December 1918.
of the Section under my
Command please

W Shipley Capt AVC
Comdg 50th Mob Vet Sect.

No. 1

WAR DIARY
or
INTELLIGENCE SUMMARY.
(Erase heading not required.)

Army Form C. 2118.

50 Mob Vety Section

December 1918

W 52 35

Place	Date	Hour	Summary of Events and Information	Remarks and references to Appendices
Tottenham	1		Daily routine wsoh	
	2		Visited No 23 Veterinary Hospital Hunt-Cont. Daily routine wsoh	
	3		Daily routine wsoh	
	4		Visited No 23 Veterinary Hospital and Hunt Row. Daily routine wsoh	
	5		Daily routine wsoh	
	6		Capt W. Shipley proceeded to U.K. on leave. Daily routine wsoh	
	7		Exercise. Daily routine wsoh	
	8		Daily routine wsoh	
	9		Daily routine wsoh	
	10		Evacuated 21 horses from No 23 Veterinary Hospital to Tottenham. Daily routine wsoh	
	11		Daily routine wsoh	
	12		Sgt White, Sgt Relf, Cpl Kony, Privs Mansfield and Harris proceeded to U.K. on leave. Daily Routine wsoh	
	13		Daily routine wsoh	
	14			

Army Form C. 2118.

WAR DIARY
or
INTELLIGENCE SUMMARY.
(Erase heading not required.)

N° 5

58 Mobile V[eterinary] Section   December 1918

Place	Date	Hour	Summary of Events and Information	Remarks and references to Appendices
Tattenham	15		Daily routine work. 16 horses & 4 men evacuated horse to Belize	
	16		" "	
	17		" "	
	18		" "	
	19		" "	
	20		" "	
	21		Capt Shipley returned from leave. Daily routine work	
	22		Daily routine work	
	23		" "	
	24		" "	
	25		" "	
	26		" "	
	27		Sgt Self returned from leave. Daily routine work	
	28		2 Lt Whyte and Cpl Looney returned from leave. Daily routine work	
	29		Driver Harris returned from leave. Daily routine work	
	30		Daily routine work	

Army Form C. 2118.

No 3
WAR DIARY
or
INTELLIGENCE SUMMARY.
(Erase heading not required.)

55 Mobile Veterinary Section December 1918.

Instructions regarding War Diaries and Intelligence Summaries are contained in F. S. Regs. Part II. Title pages will be prepared in manuscript.

Place	Date	Hour	Summary of Events and Information	Remarks and references to Appendices
Tottinghem	31		Pte Brown admitted to Hospital. Only routine work	
			W.H. Foley Capt R.A.V.C. Comdg 55 Mobile Veterinary Section	

To
D.A.G.
G.H.Q. 3rd Echelon

Herewith War Diary for
the month of January 1919
of the Section under my
command please.

W Shipley Capt RAVC
Comdg 50th Mob Vet Sect

Army Form C. 2118.

39

No. 1

WAR DIARY
or
INTELLIGENCE SUMMARY.
(Erase heading not required)

58 Motor Ambulance Convoy   January 1919   Vol 36

Instructions regarding War Diaries and Intelligence Summaries are contained in F. S. Regs., Part II. and the Staff Manual respectively. Title pages will be prepared in manuscript.

Place	Date	Hour	Summary of Events and Information	Remarks and references to Appendices
Vatubeau	1		Move to Staples. Daily routine work	
Staples	2		Move to An Wackelaine. Daily routine work	
An Wackelaine	3		3 Ambulances proceeded to U.K. on leave. Daily routine work	
"	4		Cpl Berrey and 6 men conducted 50 animals to Tournai. Daily routine work	
"	5		Cpl Berrey and 6 men conducted 50 animals to Tournai. Sgt Reef and 6 men conducted 50 animals to Courtrai. Daily routine work	
"	6		Six Ambulances proceeded to UK on leave. Daily routine work	
"	7		Section Paid. Daily routine work	
"	8		Daily routine work	
"	9		"	
"	10		"	
"	11		"	
"	12		Cpl Berrey conducted animals to Roubaix. Sk Low conducted animals to Lille. Daily routine work	
"	13		Sgt Reef and 3 men at Sale Lille 93 animals. Daily routine work	

Army Form C. 2118.

WAR DIARY
or
INTELLIGENCE SUMMARY.

(Erase heading not required.)

N° 2

50 Mille Section   Jan 1919

Instructions regarding War Diaries and Intelligence Summaries are contained in F. S. Regs., Part II. and the Staff Manual respectively. Title pages will be prepared in manuscript.

Place	Date	Hour	Summary of Events and Information	Remarks and references to Appendices
La Madeleine	14		Capt Shipley proceeded to Attrecourt, Bouton, Loft Leavy and 2 men with 8 animals to Tournai. Daily routine work.	
	15		Sgt Reef and 4 men at Sgr. LA MADELEINE 50 animals	
			Sgt Cox conducted 8 animals to LILLE to Bekke. Daily routine work	
	16		Daily routine work	
	17		— — —	
	18		Sgt Reef and 5 men at Sqn Routine 72 animals. Daily routine work.	
	19		Daily routine work	
	20		Sgt Ref at Sqn at Sqn Tournay 101 animals	
			Lpt Leavy and 2 men conducted 8 animals to Attrecourt Contrax	
			Daily routine work	
	21		Lpt Leavy and 2 men conducted 7 animals to Attrecourt Tournai	
			Lpt Cox and 2 men conducted 16 animals to Butchy at Roubaix	
			Daily routine work	
	22		Sgt Reef and 4 men at Sqr LILLE 92 animals Cpl Cox and 3 men	
			conducted 18 animals to Butchy Roubaix. Daily routine work	

N° 3

WAR DIARY
or
INTELLIGENCE SUMMARY

Army Form C. 2118.

58 Wk**** (Erase heading not required.) Section

Place	Date	Hour	Summary of Events and Information	Remarks and references to Appendices
La Madeleine	23		4 animals evacuated to M. Bonnier LILLE and 17 animals to M. DE Conset LILLE. Daily routine work	
"	24		Daily routine work	
"	25		Sgt Riley and 5 men at Sick Routine. 98 animals. Sgt Casey and 2 men evacuated 18 animals to M. Bailey Roubaix	
"	26		Daily routine work. Off Cmr and 2 men evacuated 16 animals to M. DE Conset Lille. Daily routine work	
"	27		Sgt Riley, bf Cnr & 5 men at Sick hall. 100 animals. Daily routine work. bf Com and 1 man conducted 7 animals to Veterinary Convlsnt	
"	28		Daily routine work	
"	29		- ' -	
"	30		Sgt Riley bf Cnr, 5 men at Sick Routine 102 animals. Daily routine work	
"	31		Daily routine work	

W Whipley Capt RAVC
58 Mobile Veterinary Section

www.ingramcontent.com/pod-product-compliance
Lightning Source LLC
Chambersburg PA
CBHW081539160426
43191CB00011B/1793